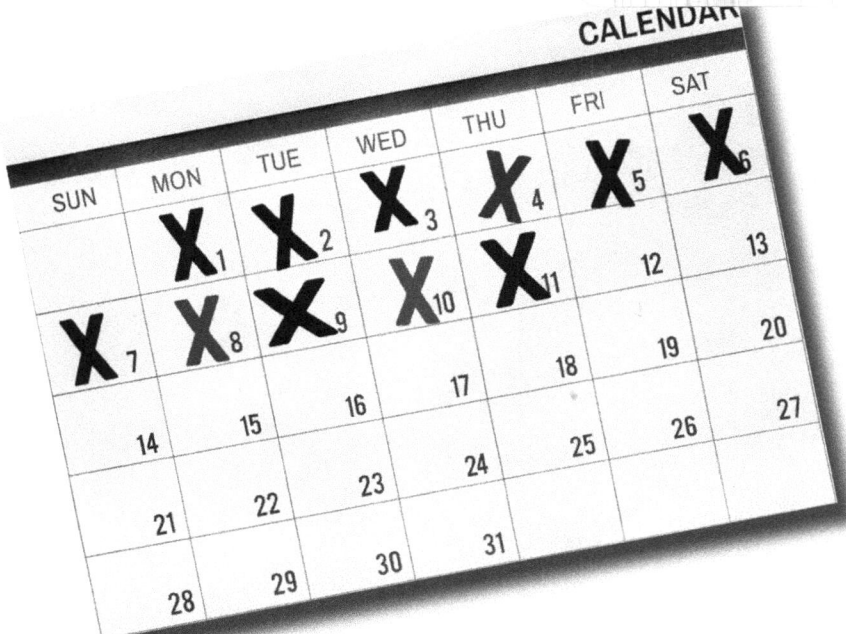

90-DAY RECOVERY GUIDE

FOR SEX & PORN ADDICTION

Mark Denison, D.Min.

Special Praise for...

90-DAY RECOVERY GUIDE FOR SEX & PORN ADDICTION

If your aim is to achieve sexual sobriety and maintain it, you must get this book today. Dr. Denison guides readers through his tried and proven approach to restoring integrity. Filled with Scripture, down-to-earth examples, and daily exercises, Dr. Denison provides a map to sobriety and a toolkit to use on the journey. This book is not only useful for those new to recovery but it gives seasoned recovery veterans the help they need to move their recovery to the next level.

Milton Magness, D.Min.
Founder, Hope & Freedom
Author of Real Hope, True Freedom

Mark has masterfully designed a powerful step-by-step set of tools to help those in bondage. I've found hope and inspiration from this 90-day guide, which has helped me break free and live the life I never thought was possible. This workbook will challenge and stretch anyone who ventures to open its pages. The work you invest in these pages will pay dividends for the rest of your life. As Mark taught me, it will work if you work it. It worked for me.

Adam White, M.D.
Philadelphia, Pennsylvania

Mark has done a phenomenal job of simplifying the difficult journey of recovery into a daily, manageable process that is proven to work. If you want to experience lifelong, everyday freedom, then dig into the pages of this book and begin applying its principles. "90-Day Recovery Guide" is thorough, practical, and life-changing.

Jonathan Daugherty
Founder of Be Broken Ministries
Author, Grace-Based Recovery

Mark has done an exceptional job in providing a map to recovery. He is clearly qualified to author this guide. Mark brings a wealth of experience from training countless numbers of people throughout the country. If you need recovery and encouragement, you need to read this book! It is a phenomenal resource for healing and sobriety, and it offers priceless tools you can use for a lifetime.

Robert McDermott
Crusade Ministries
Billy Graham Evangelistic Association

I know of no one who is more committed to the recovery of men and women who are struggling with porn and sex addiction than Mark Denison. Having found successful recovery in his own life, Mark has done the hard work of preparation for this new ministry. I highly recommend his latest work as a tool for those who long for the gift of recovery in their personal lives. This is just the beginning. Watch for more to come!

Don Bailey
Pastoral Counselor
Bradenton, Florida

For 25 years, I chased sobriety. I had lost hope, thinking sobriety was beyond my grasp. Then I found "There's Still Hope." I am living proof that the principles in this book work. I owe my recovery to the tools found in "90-Day Recovery Guide." What has worked for me will work for you!

Terry Dickson
Worship Pastor
Tampa Florida

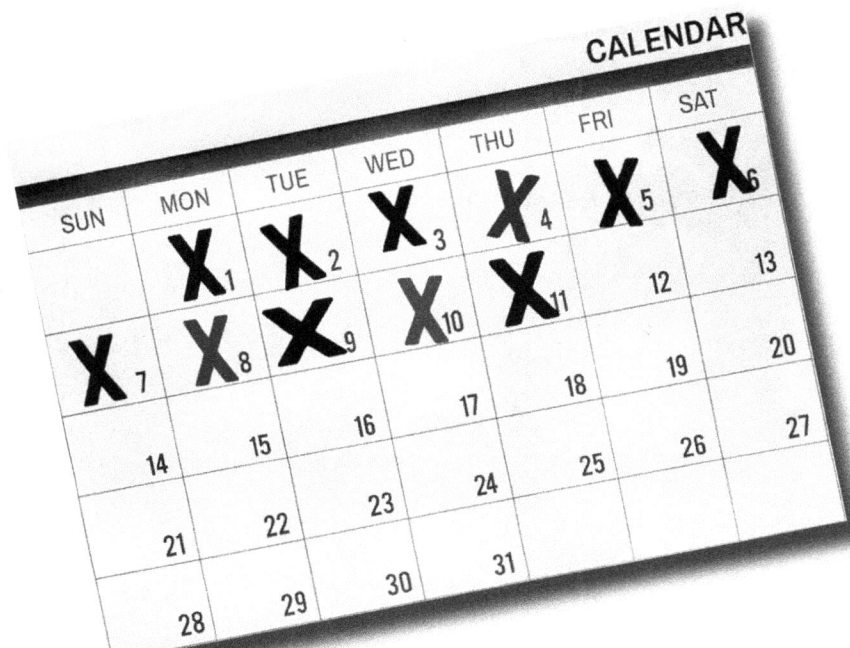

90-DAY RECOVERY GUIDE

FOR SEX & PORN ADDICTION

Mark Denison, D.Min.

www.abpbooks.com

90-Day Recovery for Sex and Porn Addiction
© Mark Denison 2018

ISBN: 978-1-7324846-5-8

Cover design by Laurie Barboza - Design Stash Books
(DesignStashBooks@gmail.com)

ALL RIGHTS RESERVED: *No part of this book may be reproduced in any form without permission in writing from the publisher, except in the case of brief quotations embodied in critical reviews or articles.*

Printed in the United States of America
2019—First Edition

*I dedicate this work to those with whom
I am blessed to share this road of recovery.*

Table of Contents

WEEK 1: Acceptance 1
    Day 1: Admit You Are Powerless 2
    Day 2: The Serenity Prayer 4
    Day 3: Own It! 6
    Day 4: Consequences 8
    Day 5: Your Sexual History 10
    Day 6: Abuse 12
    Day 7: Isolation 14

WEEK 2: Desperation 17
    Day 8: Higher Power 18
    Day 9: Desperate Times 20
    Day 10: Six Obstacles of Sobriety 22
    Day 11: Mousetraps 24
    Day 12: Get Accountable 26
    Day 13: Confront the Three 'D's 28
    Day 14: Join a 12-Step Meeting 30

WEEK 3: Goals 33
    Day 15: Define the End Game 34
    Day 16: What Life Could Be Like 36
    Day 17: Addiction Interactive Map 38
    Day 18: Red Light, Green Light 40
    Day 19: Five Causes of Your Addiction 42
    Day 20: What About Masturbation? 44
    Day 21: Recovery Day 46

WEEK 4: Surrender 49
    Day 22: The Best Decision Ever 50
    Day 23: The 3rd Step Prayer 52
    Day 24: The Addiction Cycle 54
    Day 25: What to Surrender 56

Day 26: Training the Mind...58
Day 27: Beyond the Crowd..60
Day 28: The 7th Step Prayer..62

WEEK 5: Disciplines..65
Day 29: Get in the Word...66
Day 30: Pray – Here's How..68
Day 31: The Magic of 12 Steps...70
Day 32: I Confess..72
Day 33: Once-a-Week..74
Day 34: Shape Up!..76
Day 35: The 20-Minute Rule..78

WEEK 6: Honesty..81
Day 36: Getting Honest...82
Day 37: Taking Inventory..84
Day 38: Family History..86
Day 39: Secrets..88
Day 40: Inner Circle..90
Day 41: Middle Circle...92
Day 42: Outer Circle...94

WEEK 7: Community..97
Day 43: Reconnect..98
Day 44: You Need this Guy..100
Day 45: Three Musketeers...102
Day 46: A Small Group..104
Day 47: 12-Step Group..106
Day 48: Church..108
Day 49: The Final Piece...110

WEEK 8: Triggers..113
Day 50: H.A.L.T...114
Day 51: The Loneliest Number...116
Day 52: Fantasy Island..118
Day 53: The Great Curse..120
Day 54: Bankrupted by Success..122

Day 55: The Devil's Workshop 124
Day 56: Complacency 126

WEEK 9: Guardrails 129
Day 57: The 3-Second Rule 130
Day 58: Watchman 132
Day 59: Manifesto 134
Day 60: Say No 136
Day 61: Intrusive Thoughts 138
Day 62: Get Fit 140
Day 63: Travel Plan 142

WEEK 10: Housekeeping 145
Day 64: Dump the Stash 146
Day 65: Turning the Page 148
Day 66: Realignment 150
Day 67: Good Grief 152
Day 68: Drawing Circles 154
Day 69: Letting Go 156
Day 70: Mistakes 158

WEEK 11: Disclosure 161
Day 71: Your Story 162
Day 72: Coming Clean 164
Day 73: Potter's Hand 166
Day 74: Add It Up 168
Day 75: To Tell the Truth 170
Day 76: Amends 172
Day 77: Tell All 174

WEEK 12: Maintenance 177
Day 78: Fear of Falling 178
Day 79: Gratitude 180
Day 80: Euphoric Recall 182
Day 81: Be Good to Yourself 184
Day 82: Check In 186
Day 83: Sponsoring Others 188

Day 84: Spiritual Connection..190

Finish Strong..193
   Day 85: The New You 194
   Day 86: 90-Day Check-Up..196
   Day 87: Step 12 198
   Day 88: Living Amends 200
   Day 89: Stay at It! 202
   Day 90: You Win! 204

ADDITIONAL RESOURCES 206

SUGGESTED READINGS..207

ABOUT THE AUTHOR 209

PREFACE

Congratulations! You are reading this because you have made a commitment to recovery from sex and porn addiction. You are one of a growing number who have fallen captive to the seduction of Internet pornography and many other forms of sexually compulsive behaviors.

There are many facets to successful recovery: therapy, 12-step work, recovery groups, reading appropriate materials, inpatient and outpatient services, three-day intensives, workshops, and spiritual disciplines. Although all of these are important ingredients to sobriety, we have found three components to recovery that are indispensable, and that, when blended, offer the best opportunity for success. This workbook integrates all three.

1. A disciplined plan

Few find lasting sobriety apart from a disciplined plan. This 90-day workbook provides that plan. Within these pages you will find 90 daily exercises that incorporate the latest research and accepted principles that lead to successful recovery. Although we embrace the 12 steps, this is not a 12-step program. We build your recovery around 12 tested pillars. For the next 90 days, you will spend a week on each of these 12 pillars of recovery.

2. A spiritual program

In 12-step work you will hear a lot about a "Higher Power." We believe that power is God, experienced personally through his son, Jesus Christ. You are welcome to pursue your Higher Power apart from the Christian faith, but you will find dozens of Scriptures and biblical references throughout this book. Unlike other recovery plans, we have included one devotional for each of the 90 days, corresponding with that daily exercise.

3. Personal coaching

Studies confirm that, while books, conferences, and meetings all play a vital role in recovery, nothing takes the place of one-on-one coaching. That is what we offer at There's Still Hope. This workbook is not intended to be completed on your own. For the most successful outcome, you need a personal guide who has been there and is trained in assisting others in their recovery. Our team provides that service at an affordable rate. I commit 20 hours a week to coach others myself.

Again, there are a lot of good resources on the market. But we believe that our confluence of a 90-day plan, spiritual program, and personal coaching sets you up for the most success. This will not be easy. If you want to attend a meeting now and then, and drop in on a counselor when the crisis hits – but not engage a daily plan for recovery – this is not for you.

But I'm guessing you have already tried half-hearted measures and found them lacking. That's how you found us.

The good news is that sex and porn addiction is treatable. And although 90 days of sobriety cannot guarantee you a lifetime of recovery, this can be the start that you desperately need. But as we say in 12-step meetings, it will only work if you work it. If you are ready to get well, you will need to commit 20 minutes a day to this process – for the next 90 days.

Think of it like this. What you desperately long for is a whole new world called recovery. To get there, you need three things: a rocket, fuel, and a pilot. We provide all three. So if you are ready to discover that world you have always dreamed of, we can help. We offer the rocket (90-day plan), fuel (spiritual connection), and pilot (our team).

Let's get started . . .

ACKNOWLEDGMENTS

This work is, in large part, a product of my own recovery. I would be remiss if I did not acknowledge just a few of the saints God has used to lead me to the great discovery of recovery.

First, I am most grateful for Beth, my beautiful wife. She is simply the godliest person I know. Every day, I have a front row seat to witness the character of Christ in a person saved by grace. She is my partner in ministry and my best friend.

I am indebted to my pastor and spiritual father. Dr. Cecil Sewell led me to faith in Christ, and remains, well into his 80s, my advisor, mentor, and friend. Dr. Sewell is a true throwback – a gifted preacher with the heart of a shepherd.

I must acknowledge my favorite professor. Dr. Gene Wofford taught me more with his life than he did as my instructor. And that's saying a lot, given that I took every class he taught at Houston Baptist University.

There are too many men to list, who have walked with me on my personal journey of recovery. I have been blessed to have the best sponsor ever, and am grateful for all the men in my 12-step groups.

Finally, this work would not have happened apart from the endless mentoring and encouragement Beth and I have received from Dr. Milton Magness and his wife Kathie. The long conversations, dinners in their home, and priceless direction can never be repaid.

WEEK 1

ACCEPTANCE

"Happiness can exist only in acceptance."
 - George Orwell

Day 1: Admit You Are Powerless

God's Word for Today

On December 11, 1934, Bill took his last drink. He brought his message of sobriety to his friend, Dr. Bob, who took his last drink on June 10, 1935. Together, the two men embraced their own powerlessness over alcohol – and Alcoholics Anonymous was birthed.

The first step in overcoming addiction is to acknowledge that we are powerless over our disease. Until we admit our disease has us whipped and that there is nothing we can do to overcome it in our own strength, we cannot get well.

One day Jesus climbed out of a boat, only to be greeted by a man whose life was out of control. After calming a storm, Jesus was ready to calm a heart. But to say the man was inconsolable is an understatement. The Bible says, "This man lived in the burial caves and could no longer be restrained" (Mark 5:3).

> *"A good man can be stupid and still be good."*

The man could not be bound. But while he had great strength, he was too weak to stop his self-inflicting behavior. He was completely powerless to do anything about it.

Porn and sex addiction are more than a moral dilemma. Russian author Maxim Gorky said it well. "A good man can be stupid and still be good." This addiction cannot be overcome by resistance, remorse, or repentance.

Addiction takes us further than we want to go, keeps us longer than we want to stay, and costs us more than we want to pay. Still, we continue in our self-destructive behaviors because that's what addicts do. But there is hope – once we admit our powerlessness over our disease.

Today's Exercise

We all thought we could lick this problem on our own. But if you could overcome porn and sex addiction in your own strength, you wouldn't be reading this right now. You would have stopped years ago - before it cost you your marriage, job, reputation, or all three. I'll say what I think you already know - work doesn't work, no matter how good that work may be.

You are powerless, and the sooner you admit that, the sooner you will recover. Successful recovery is spiritual recovery. And it does not take place in a vacuum. You need to take others with you for the journey, starting today.

Step 1 says, "We admitted we were powerless over lust and that our lives had become unmanageable."

Admitted to whom?

The answer is twofold — God and one other person.

You Are Powerless — Tell Someone

1. State your powerlessness over sex or porn addiction in your own words: _____
   _____
   _____

2. Now, pause and tell God. Pray something like this: "God, I admit it. I have a struggle with addiction that I cannot win by myself. I am powerless to overcome this on my own."

3. Now, write the name of one person with whom you will share your addiction: _____

Day 2: The Serenity Prayer

God's Word for Today

Robin Williams, who fought addiction his entire life, said wryly, "Reality is just a crutch for people who can't cope with drugs." He had a point. The sooner we accept the reality we did not choose, the sooner we get well.

In preparation for a sermon at the Heath Evangelical Union Church in Heath, Massachusetts, in 1934, Reinhold Niebuhr wrote this prayer: *"God, grant me the serenity to accept the things I cannot change, the courage to change the things I can, and the wisdom to know the difference."*

First published in a magazine in 1951, the Serenity Prayer has become a staple for 12-step programs of all kinds. This gem begins with a plea to accept one's weakness.

"It is in our weakness that we find God's strength."

It is in our weakness that we find God's strength. King David understood this when he wrote, "God knows how we are formed; he remembers that we are dust" (Psalm 102:14).

You did not ask for your addiction, nor can you wish it away. To accept your addiction is not a sign of weakness, but of strength.

D.L. Moody said it like this: "The definition of faith is placing your weakness into God's strength."

Three times, the Apostle Paul prayed that God would remove his personal, unique, unwanted affliction. And all three times, God said no. Late in his life, writing from prison, Paul said, "I have learned in whatever state I am to be content" (Philippians 4:11).

Recovery begins by accepting the reality of our struggle. Start by praying what millions have prayed before: *"God, grant me the serenity to accept the things I cannot change . . ."*

Today's Exercise

You remember what you write. In a 2014 study done by the Association of Psychological Science, it was found that students who take notes receive a memory boost.[1] A similar study by Indiana University in 2010 concluded that the areas of the brain associated with learning work far better when we write things out.

Memorize the Serenity Prayer. Start by writing it out below.

"God, grant me the serenity to accept the things I cannot change, the courage to change the things I can, and the wisdom to know the difference."

_____
_____
_____
_____

Now, answer this question. If you could accept the reality of your addiction to porn or sex, how might this make your life better? List three ways:

1. _____
2. _____
3. _____

---

1 K. Ismail, "6 Psychological Benefits of Writing Things Down," July 4, 2016, blog.

Day 3: Own It!

God's Word for Today

Samuel L. Jackson, a recovering addict, said, "I guess the worst day I have had was when I had to stand up in rehab in front of my wife and daughter and say, 'Hi, my name is Sam, and I am an addict.'"

One of the early building blocks to recovery is ownership. We must own our addiction.

From the first man of creation until now, this has been a struggle. After Adam had disobeyed God, his Creator confronted him about what he had done.

"Why did you eat the forbidden fruit?" God asked him. Adam's response has reverberated through the corridors of time.

> *"Until we take ownership for our disease, we will never take responsibility for our recovery."*

"The woman you put here with me – she gave me some fruit from the tree, and I ate it" (Genesis 3:12).

With a single statement, Adam managed to implicate his wife and his God. It wasn't enough that he blamed Eve. Notice how he said it. He called her "the woman you put here with me."

I don't recall much of a protest the day God presented Eve to Adam. But now that he stumbled, his addiction to fruit and pride was not only Eve's fault; it was God's. If God hadn't created Eve, Adam would have been just fine. Talk about insanity!

Many of us blame others for our disease. We blame our mother, our father, a teacher, a bully, the baker and candlestick maker. We even blame our God.

Here's what many addicts never come to accept. Until we take ownership for our disease, we will not take responsibility for our recovery. Let me be blunt. This is your addiction. Own it or it will own you – for the rest of your life.

Today's Exercise

We are all a product of our pasts. I have yet to meet a man or woman who said, "I chose this addiction." But the truth is this: until you take ownership of your disease, you will never take responsibility for your recovery.

It is likely that sources beyond your control contributed to your addiction. Your family history, childhood trauma, and early isolation all came together to form the perfect storm. But now it's *your storm, your addiction, your disease – your responsibility*.

It's time to own your problem, because you are ultimately the only one who can do anything about it. Acceptance is the foundation of recovery, and owning your problem is a building block of acceptance.

Take a moment and answer these questions.

1. In what ways have you contributed to your disease/addiction?
   _____
   _____
   _____
   _____

2. What are some things you have done since you knew you had a problem that only made things worse?
   _____
   _____
   _____

3. What are some recovery tools that you have failed to put in place?
   _____
   _____
   _____

Day 4: Consequences

God's Word for Today

You make your choices, then your choices make you. In your addiction, you get to pick your decisions, but not your consequences. For every mistake there is a price to pay. But don't worry – you are in good company. We have all messed up from time to time.

I know a church in Alabama that calls itself "the church for messed up people." Another church in Atlanta dubs itself "the perfect church for people who aren't." The truth is, we are all messed up, imperfect souls. In fact, the Bible is full of messed up people – who still did great things.

Noah got drunk and exposed himself to his sons. Abraham lied about his wife and slept with her maid.

"You make your choices, then your choices make you."

Jacob deceived his blind father. Moses killed an Egyptian he had never met. Gideon had 70 sons with his wives and another son with his girlfriend. Abimelech killed all 70 of his half-brothers. Peter denied Jesus three times. Paul dragged Christians through the city streets.

King David goes to the head of the messed-up class of messed-up people. He slept with another man's wife, then had the man killed so he could take the woman as his bride. But the pleasure of the moment led to the loss of a lifetime. David's sin cost him his son.

But we serve a God of redemption. Despite David's sexual brokenness and sin, he would be recognized by God as "a man after my own heart" (Acts 13:22).

Yes, God uses messed up people. He can mop up your biggest mess. You are exactly the kind of person God uses. So bring your *messed up* life to your *clean up* God. For every sin there is a consequence, and for every sinner there is grace.

Today's Exercise

We are sinners because we sin and we sin because we are sinners. We are all messed up. But for this disease there is hope in Jesus Christ. Falling into addiction was not a choice; remaining in it is. Because of the recovery tools that are available, those who remain in their old lifestyle are "without excuse" (Romans 1:20).

If you ever engage in a three-day intensive with a Certified Sex Addiction Therapist (CSAT), you will be asked to chronicle all that your addiction has cost you – in lost relationships, time, resources, and reputation. It is a staggering exercise. But until you realize how far you have fallen, you are unlikely to get up.

So take a few minutes and jot down some of the consequences of your addiction.

1. Lost or damaged relationships: _____
   _____
   _____
   _____

2. Other problems caused by your addiction: _____
   _____
   _____
   _____
   _____

Day 5: Your Sexual History

God's Word for Today

You have a sexual history – some good, some bad. We all do. And your sexual history has led you down the road of addiction. That begs the question . . .

Once an addict, always an addict? That is a question that has been debated for years. My intention is not to answer that question, other than to say that God is the master at using our pasts.

There was a man in the Bible who hosted Jesus and a group of his friends in his home one day. His name was Simon, better known as "Simon the Leper." The Scripture tells us, "Jesus was in Bethany in the home of Simon the Leper" (Matthew 26:6).

> *"God won't use you despite your past, but because of it."*

We can assume that Simon was actually no longer a leper, or he would not have been allowed in the presence of crowds, as leprosy was thought to be highly contagious and deadly. Clearly, Simon was a former leper. Yet he still identified with his past.

God doesn't want you to run from your past. In fact, he won't use you despite your past, but because of it. Your past becomes God's purpose and your problem becomes your platform.

As a former pastor, it took me awhile to get comfortable with the idea of leading from my past. Being known can be scary. We often embrace the falsehood that our past invalidates our future.

Lisa Bevere wrote, "If you think you've blown God's plan for your life, rest in this. You, my friend, are not that powerful."

You have a past. We all do. But here's the good news. Your past is not a deterrent to God using you in the future; rather, it opens up new opportunities you never knew existed before.

Today's Exercise

Patrick Carnes has given us a great tool of insight into the history of our sexual brokenness, with *Facing the Shadows*. He suggests that we answer 13 questions in defining our personal history of sexual addiction. Some of the following questions are adapted from his work.[2]

1. At what age did you first view pornography? _____

2. What traumatic events led to your sexual brokenness early in life?
   a. _____
   b. _____
   c. _____

3. How did your sexual addiction originally manifest itself?
   _____
   _____

4. In what ways has it escalated?
   a. _____
   b. _____
   c. _____

5. What "acting out" behavior do you struggle with the most?
   _____

6. What is the behavior for which you are most ashamed?
   _____

---

2   Patrick Carnes, *Facing the Shadow: Starting Sexual and Relationship Recovery*, Third Edition (Center City, NV: Hazelden, 2015), 105-107.

Day 6: Abuse

God's Word for Today

Current data on sex abuse among children is daunting. David Finkelhor, Director of the Crimes Against Children Research Center, has conducted studies that show that one in five girls has been a victim of sexual abuse. Another study reveals that 28 percent of those ages 14 to 17 have been sexually abused.[3]

Abuse robs us of our innocence. It puts our sexual integrity and sanity at risk. In the past of nearly every addict is abuse, sexual or otherwise. But as painful as it is, the addict must learn to turn the page and move forward.

Getting beyond the pain is never easy. Consider the case of Abraham. At the age of 137, he lost his beloved wife. Part of Abraham died with her. After Sarah's death came a period of mourning. Then Abraham buried his wife and moved on.

"Your mountain is waiting, so get on your way."

Yes, after he buried his wife, "Abraham moved on" (Genesis 20:1). He lived another 38 years, and even remarried. The man suffered enormous pain, but he moved on.

One of the hardest things for any of us to do in light of abuse or pain is to move on. But here's the tough lesson: while getting hurt is not a choice, getting stuck is.

The first time I visited the Magnolia Market at the silos of Chip and Joanna Gaines, I saw a sign. I had to have it. (I like to pretend Chip hand-carved it just for me!) Now hanging on my wall at home, it reads, "Your mountain is waiting, so get on your way."

This is a message for every addict and spouse. Yesterday's crisis opens the door to tomorrow's blessings. But you have to walk through that door. "Your mountain is waiting, so get on your way."

---

3   D. Finkelhor, National Center for Victims of Crime, website.

Today's Exercise

Psychotherapist Nathaniel Brandon said, "The first step toward change is awareness."

Understandably, many sexual and porn addicts have stuffed the baggage of their past, including horrific events of abuse. But until we face the giants of our past, we cannot defeat them.

Like Abraham, you must identify the source of your pain in order to "move on." Patrick Carnes' groundbreaking book, *Out of the Shadows*,[4] offers a template for identifying our abuse, in order that we might deal with it.

1. Sexual abuse: list the ways you have been sexually abused in the past, when these events occurred, and who the perpetrators were.
    a. _____
    b. _____
    c. _____

2. Physical abuse: list the ways you have been physically abused in the past, when these events occurred, and who the perpetrators were.
    a. _____
    b. _____
    c. _____

3. Emotional abuse: list the ways you have been emotionally abused in the past, when these events occurred, and who the perpetrators were.
    a. _____
    b. _____
    c. _____

---

4 Patrick Carnes, *Out of the Shadows: Understanding Sexual Addiction*, Third Edition. (Center City, NV: Hazelden, 2012), 104-105.

Day 7: Isolation

God's Word for Today

Pitcairn Island is one of the most remote places on earth. Set in the Pacific Ocean, it is home to just 50 residents, and for good reason – you can't get there. You must fly to Tahiti and then sail for 1,200 miles. Then you transfer to a dinghy, take your climbing gear, and eventually scale the 900-foot rock cliffs to the tiny village.

Pitcairn Island is a metaphor for loneliness and isolation. And Pitcairn Island is a metaphor for addiction.

Solomon wrote, "Whoever isolates himself seeks his own desire; he rejects sound judgment" (Proverbs 18:1).

> *"Isolation is not a condition as much as it is a choice."*

Addicts come in all shapes and sizes. Addiction knows no color or creed, race or religion. But if you look hard enough and long enough into every addict's past you will find the same thing.

Isolation.

Hear the words of John Lennon's hit song from 1970: *"People say we've got it made. Don't they know we're so afraid? We're afraid to be alone. Everybody got to have a home."*

The facts are these. Nobody has it made, we're all afraid, we don't want to be alone, and we've all got to have a home.

Here's the thing. Isolation is not a condition as much as it is a choice. So, join the family of God, get in a support group, and get outside yourself. Why? Because if you don't defeat the demon of isolation, the demon of isolation will defeat you.

Today's Exercise

At the root of every addiction is isolation. We may not even know it, but it is there – hidden away, like a dark secret nobody knows. You may have been driven into isolation by abuse, a handicap, or parental neglect. To find the source of your isolation, you must dig deep.

List the causes of your isolation.

1. Abuse: _____
2. Handicap: _____
3. Neglect: _____

Most addicts continue to isolate. They fear being fully known. "Would anyone love me if they really knew me?" they ask. The good news is that in effective recovery, we begin to break down the walls of isolation. We build meaningful relationships. Here are a few ways to build the relationships that will break the stranglehold of isolation. Check the ones you have engaged, and start working on the rest.

1. Join a 12-step group _____
2. Get a sponsor _____
3. Get three phone numbers from fellow 12-step members _____
4. Build a circle of five accountability partners _____
5. Join a church or Bible Study group _____

WEEK 2

DESPERATION

*"I don't think human beings learn anything until
they are desperate."*
- Jim Carrey

Day 8: Higher Power

God's Word for Today

Jesus came upon a man who had been a cripple for 38 years. We can assume the paralytic had tried everything: doctors, religion, and home remedies. Still he could not walk. He had played his last card and was out of options. So he looked to Jesus.

Then Jesus asked him the strangest question. "Do you want to be well?" (John 5:6). Was that a serious question? Of course he wanted to be well. Who wouldn't?

But Jesus' question really wasn't one of desire, but desperation. "Do you *really* want to be well?" Then Jesus told the man to pick up his mat and walk. That required the willingness to play the part of a fool. What if he picked up his mat, but then the healing didn't really take place?

> *"When we do the improbable, God does the impossible."*

But when he did the improbable (picked up his mat), God did the impossible. And the man was healed.

This week we are talking about the second building block to recovery – desperation. Unfortunately, most of us are more comfortable with the problem we know than the solution we don't. As a consequence, we never find freedom.

Real breakthrough only happens when we are truly desperate to touch God and have him touch us. We must seek his presence more than his blessings.

St. Augustine said, "To fall in love with God is the greatest romance; to seek him the greatest adventure; to find him, the greatest human achievement."

Perhaps – like the man in our story – you have been mired in years of pain and struggle. The answer is found in a question. Do you want to be well – *really*?

Today's Exercise

When we do the improbable, God does the impossible. In the devotional you just read, Jesus asked the question we all must confront. "Do you want to be well?" The original text reads more strongly. "Do you *really* want to be well?"

What came after the healing is important. Jesus found the man in the temple. There was something within him that said, "I've got to connect with God." That's where the magic begins – with a relationship with God. Recovery is a spiritual journey.

So I ask you, in the midst of your struggle – *Do you want to get well – really?*

To get well you must connect with your Higher Power. That's what today's lesson is about. To be desperate to be well is to be desperate for God. Here are some ways to do this . . .

1. Pray the 3rd Step Prayer: "God, I offer myself to you, to build with me and do with me as you will. Relieve me of the bondage of self, that I may better do your will. Take away my difficulties, that victory over them may bear witness to those I would help of your power, your love, and your way of life."

2. In your own words, reach out to God. Tell him how desperate you are to win your battle with addiction and to connect with him.

3. Take a hard look at your life. Confess your character defects and sins. Ask for God's forgiveness and the power to live for him today.

Day 9: Desperate Times

God's Word for Today

The ancient Greek physician Hippocrates is credited with the phrase, "Desperate times call for desperate measures." And addiction calls for desperate measures.

The Old Testament tells us the story of a powerful man who was rendered helpless by his unwanted disease. Only when he became desperate did he get well.

As an Aramean army commander, Naaman was an imposing military and political figure. He had power, position, and prosperity. But he also had leprosy, which was a horrific disease that branded its victim a lonely outcast from everything he knew. Naaman knew his destiny – a slow, painful, lonely death.

> *"Only when he became desperate did he get well."*

Naaman became desperate. He heard about a prophet named Elisha who had healed multitudes. So he found the prophet and asked to be healed. Elisha ordered the commander to dip himself in the muddy Jordan River seven times. Say what? This was unbecoming for a man of Naaman's stature, so he did what most of us would have done. He went away angry – and still sick.

Naaman thought about it and was moved to desperation – to the point of doing whatever it took to be well. It was when he acknowledged his powerlessness over his disease that he followed Elisha's instructions. Only then was he made whole.

The question is not if you want to overcome your addiction, but how badly you want it. There is a common phrase in 12-step work. "Half measures availed us nothing." You can get well. But first, you must get desperate.

Today's Exercise

Are you desperate to be well? Then there can be nothing taken off the table. Most of us are happy to take the recovery steps that come easy to us. But it is the steps that make you uncomfortable that will serve you best.

Patrick Carnes has done extensive research on the things that work in addiction recovery. He concludes, "The people who had the greatest success took the same steps in a relatively predictable fashion. Out of our research an overall pattern emerged."[5]

Carnes then offered nine recovery activities, which are listed below. Check the ones you are willing to do, if necessary. And remember, the activities you want to do least will probably produce the best results.

1. See a therapist _____

2. Join a therapy group _____

3. Attend a 12-step meeting every week _____

4. Address other addictions _____

5. Identify family-of-origin issues _____

6. Involve family in early therapy _____

7. Have spouse attend 12-step meetings _____

8. Develop a spiritual life _____

9. Maintain a healthy diet and exercise consistently _____

---

[5] Carnes, *Facing the Shadows*, 302-303.

Day 10: Six Obstacles of Sobriety

God's Word for Today

F.B. Meyer said, "We must get to the end of ourselves before God can begin in us."

Teddy Roosevelt said it like this: "When you reach the end of your rope, tie a knot and hang on."

Every person I know who has experienced successful recovery has one thing in common: they first hit bottom.

The Bible tells the story of one such woman. Her husband had just died, and she was struggling to provide for her children. She feared that she might lose them to slavery, as was common in that day. She had precious few resources and her family was hungry. In her desperation, the woman called for the local preacher, Elisha. The prophet's first response was to focus, not on what she had lost, but on what she had left.

> *"We must get to the end of ourselves before God can begin in us."*

The widow had a little bit of oil. "She went and told the man of God, and he said, 'Go, sell the oil and pay off your debts. You and your sons can live on what is left'" (2 Kings 4:7). In obedience, she started to fill the jars with oil, and God miraculously multiplied her resources.

Don't miss that. When the widow poured out what little she had left, God stepped in – after she hit bottom.

If you have hit bottom, know this: that's a good place to be. Why? Because when you have played your last card, God steps in with a whole new deck.

Today's Exercise

Thomas Hobbes said, "Hell is truth seen too late." The problem for many sexual addicts is that they see the truth, but not in time. And the unseen truth is that (a) they have a problem, and (b) it takes hard work to sustain recovery.

Milton Magness identifies six obstacles to sobriety in his groundbreaking workbook, *Thirty Days to Hope & Freedom*.[6] Recognizing these obstacles is not difficult; dealing with them is. And you probably won't do that – unless you are desperate.

Here are six obstacles to recovery. Write a one sentence response to each, by stating how you intend to counter each obstacle.

1. Isolation: _____

2. Dishonesty: _____

3. Secrecy: _____

4. Selfishness: _____

5. Denial: _____

6. Resistance: _____

---

[6] Milton Magness, *Thirty Days to Hope & Freedom* (Las Vegas, NV: Central Recovery Press, 2012), 11-16.

Day 11: Mousetraps

God's Word for Today

Every person who has fallen into sin has the same story. It is the story of Lot, nephew of Abraham. When their families became too big their territory became too small. They agreed to go their separate ways. Lot got to pick which land would be his.

The Bible says, "Lot cast his tent toward Sodom" (Genesis 13:12). It took exactly one chapter for Lot to complete his relocation. In just a few days Lot moved from near Sodom to in Sodom (Genesis 14:12), and this one bad move nearly cost him everything.

There's an old proverb that says, "Free cheese is always available in mousetraps." Lot got in trouble because he chose to hang around a big mousetrap where he could sniff the cheese.

"Free cheese is always available in the mousetrap."

The key to staying sexually pure is to avoid that which is sexually impure. Block the channel. Delete the phone number. Change the route. End the relationship.

Avoid the mousetrap.

Each of us who has fallen really has the same story. I have yet to meet the man who said, "I viewed porn in order to wreck my marriage." The enemy doesn't tempt us that way. Had someone walked up to Lot and said, "Hey, why don't you move to Sodom, the most wicked place on earth?" he would have surely turned away.

The temptation is to camp on the hill near Sodom, to smile at the new lady at work, or to quickly browse the Internet site. And then – in an instant – we fall. Like Lot, we never meant to go all in. We only meant to sniff the cheese.

There is only one answer. Avoid the mousetrap.

Today's Exercise

There is no limit to the number of "mousetraps" the enemy sets for each of us. And in every trap is a different cheese, one that appeals to the mouse in question. You have different triggers than I do, and my struggles are different from yours. But there lies in front of all of us the traps that stand ready to snap our sobriety without a moment's notice.

Let's consider three categories of mousetraps each of us must face. Take a few minutes and list the various traps you face in each category. Then learn from the parable of the mousetrap and run the other way. Remember, the distance from near Sodom to in Sodom is very short.

We all have struggles in these three areas. What traps do you need to avoid?

1. Places
    a. _____
    b. _____
    c. _____

2. People
    a. _____
    b. _____
    c. _____

3. Predicaments
    a. _____
    b. _____
    c. _____

Day 12: Get Accountable

God's Word for Today

Tucked away in the Book of Judges is the story of a man named Jephthah. The Bible says, "Then the Spirit of the Lord came on Jephthah. He crossed Gilead and Manasseh, passed through Mizpah of Gilead, and from there he advanced against the Ammonites. And Jephthah made a vow to the Lord: If you give me the Ammonites into my hands, whatever comes out of the door of my house to meet me when I return in triumph from the Ammonites will be the Lord's, and I will sacrifice it as a burnt offering" (Judges 11:29-32).

This commander of God's army made this vow and he stuck with it. God's victory would be followed by man's sacrifice.

Ecclesiastes 5:4 says, "When you make a vow to God, do not delay to fulfill it."

What vows have you made to God? Have you said something like this? "God, if you bless me with (fill in the blank), I will never view inappropriate websites again." That is a vow worth keeping.

"The key to your sobriety is not to make new promises to God and others. They are waiting for you to keep the promises you have already made."

Robert Frost famously wrote, "The woods are lovely, dark and deep. But I have promises to keep, and miles to go before I sleep."

Before you walk your next mile – or step – think about the promises you have made to God, your spouse, and others. Be like Jephthah. Keep your word as surely as God has kept his.

The key to your sobriety is not to make new promises to God and others. They are waiting for you to keep the promises you have already made.

Today's Exercise

One study suggests that only one person in 10,000 finds sobriety on his own. We need others. And we need accountability. To whom are you accountable today?

There are several steps you can take to help. Get on Covenant Eyes. If you are still in contact with your acting out partners, change your cell number and your personal email address. Get off Facebook. Get active in a 12-step group such as Sexaholics Anonymous (SA), Sex Addicts Anonymous (SAA), or Celebrate Recovery (CR), and get a sponsor. Offer to do a full disclosure – with a polygraph – for your spouse. Ask your spouse what other things you can do to rebuild trust.

Are you serious about recovery? Then sign this covenant, between you and God.

Today, _____ (date), I make a commitment to end every affair and destructive relationship. I will become accountable for my actions by doing whatever is necessary. With the input of my spouse (if married), I agree in advance to change my cell number, to change my email address, and to get off Facebook. I will join a 12-step group and get a sponsor. I agree to give a full disclosure, if asked to do so. I further commit to doing anything else that will ensure accountability in my personal life.

Signed _____

Day 13: Confront the Three 'D's

God's Word for Today

A few years ago, Lindsay Lohan said, "I'm 20 years old. I like to party as much as anyone my age. Going clubbing is my way of relaxing or releasing a lot of stress. I don't feel that I should have to justify that part of my life. I don't know that I'm necessarily an addict."

One of the early building blocks to recovery is a transcendent desire for recovery. We must come to the place where we scream, "I want it! I must have it! I'm willing to pay any price and go to any length to find it!"

At the heart of recovery is a desire that eats away at our insides until we take the necessary steps to get well. We can't play around with our addiction with words like, "I don't know that I'm necessarily an addict."

> *"What we desire today is what we pour ourselves into tomorrow."*

The Bible promises us, "Take delight in the Lord, and he will give you the desires of your heart" (Psalm 37:4).

What we desire today is what we pour ourselves into tomorrow. And what we pour ourselves into tomorrow will shape the rest of our lives.

Is your desire for purity strong enough to fight through the pain in order to find recovery? Recovery is about desire. Mario Andretti was asked the key to success. He answered, "It's all about desire."

In recovery, it's all about desire. You can get well – but only if you want it more than anything else in the world.

Today's Exercise

When Jesus confronted men and women in need, he spoke to three things. Here are some quick examples. I call them the three 'D's.

Recovery requires death. When Lazarus was sick, Jesus said his sickness would not end in death. Lazarus still died, but it didn't end there. When there is death, God goes to work. At the end of every death awaits a resurrection.

Recovery requires disclosure. When Jesus encountered the woman at the well, their conversation quickly went to her past relationships. She came clean. She had been married five times, and was now living with a man who was not her husband.

Recovery requires desire. Remember what Jesus said to the man who was a cripple for 38 years? "Do you really want to be well?" Only when the man did the improbable (pick up his mat) could Jesus do the impossible (healing). There is no recovery without desire.

Are you ready to fully embrace these three 'D's? Answer "Yes" or "No" for each one.

1. Death: I am ready to die to my past, my selfish desires, and all that stands in the way of recovery.   Yes _____   No _____

2. Disclosure: I am willing to do a full disclosure, including a polygraph; no more secrets.   Yes _____   No _____

3. Desire: I will put my desire for sobriety and recovery above all else.   Yes _____   No _____

Day 14: Join a 12-Step Meeting

God's Word for Today

G.K. Chesterton said, "Every man who knocks on the door of a brothel is looking for God."

The biochemical model of addiction tells us why competent, intelligent people can easily be sidetracked by their pursuit of sex. Dr. Michael Herkov writes, "Studies indicate that food, abused drugs, and sexual interests share a common pathway within our brains' survival and reward systems. This pathway leads into the area of the brain responsible for our rational thoughts and judgment."

Robert Weiss, founder of The Sexual Recovery Institute, says, "What sex addiction is really about is an intimacy disorder."

In other words, there is something deeper than sex that drives the addict to his bottom line behaviors. That is why the addiction is often referred to as "cunning and baffling" in sex addiction literature.

"Addiction is not just a bad problem; it's a bad solution."

So what is the answer? For the addict, his addiction is not just a bad problem. It's a bad solution. He is knocking on the wrong door, searching for a God he may not even know exists. And the whole time, God is seeking him. That's where surrender comes into play. The addict's intimacy vacuum can only be filled by God.

Hear God's voice. "Here I am! I stand at the door and knock. If anyone hears my voice and opens the door, I will come in and eat with that person, and he with me" (Revelation 3:20).

In your search of happiness, you have knocked on the wrong door. But there is hope. Someone is now knocking on your door. Open the door and let him in. That is the key to lasting peace and recovery.

Today's Exercise

In today's devotion, we talked about knocking on the wrong door. Let's talk about one of the right doors – the hardest door for many of us to approach. I'm talking about the door to your first 12-step meeting.

I still remember when I knocked on my first door. Once inside, I was surrounded by a bunch of sex addicts. "What a bunch of weirdos," I thought. It took me far too long to realize that I am one of those "weirdos."

Research on sexual addiction confirms that nothing is more powerful on the road to recovery than joining a 12-step group.

In *Real Hope, True Freedom*, Milton Magness and Marsha Means point to 12-step work as the initial component to successful sobriety.[7]

This week's theme has been "desperation." If you are truly desperate for recovery, it's time to attend your first 12-step group, if you have not done so already. I have listed several options below. Your assignment for today is to find a local group, and then go as soon as possible.

1. Sexaholics Anonymous (www.sa.org)

2. Sex Addicts Anonymous (www.saa-recovery.org)

3. Sex and Love Addicts Anonymous (www.slaafws.org)

4. Sexual Compulsives Anonymous (www.sca-recovery.org)

5. Sexual Recovery Anonymous (www.sexualrecovery.org)

6. Celebrate Recovery (www.celebraterecovery.com)

---

7   Milton Magness and Marsha Means, *Real Hope, True Freedom: Understanding and Coping with Sex Addiction* (Las Vegas, NV: Central Recovery Press, 2017), 75.

WEEK 3

GOALS

*"Set your goals high, and don't stop
until you get there."*
- Bo Jackson

Day 15: Define the End Game

God's Word for Today

Jesus said, "Where your treasure is, there will your heart be also" (Matthew 6:21).

This week we are talking about goals. In order to find lasting recovery, that must become your treasure, your end game. You must seek sobriety with laser focus.

Warren Buffet has an interesting take on investments. He said, "Diversification is for people who don't know what they're doing." In other words, you must have a plan and stick to it. Never lose your focus. When we diversify our heart – it's called compartmentalizing – we lose our way, and our sobriety.

If you have made a mess of things, don't fret. It's never too late to set new goals. Remember, we serve the God who invented second chances.

Carl Bard wrote, "Though no one can go back and make a brand new start, anyone can start now and make a brand new ending."

> *"Though no one can go back and make a brand new start, anyone can start now and make a brand new ending."*

What will your ending look like? What you did yesterday is history. What you do today is a choice. God has given you a whole new set of choices to make today. And after you make your choices, your choices will make you. So proceed with caution. Think big, but start small.

Live today with the end game in mind. You have set goals for your finances, weight, and family. Now set clear, attainable goals for your sobriety. God has given you a fresh start. Your future awaits.

Today's Exercise

When we set goals, a good framework is the S.M.A.R.T. method, first introduced in the November 1981 issue of *Management Review*, by George T. Doran.[8] Adapted by Peter Drucker, we are encouraged to set goals that are specific, measurable, attainable, relevant, and timely.

For today's exercise, set some recovery goals. Make sure they meet all five criteria. Set goals for the short-term, mid-term, and long-term. Short-term means the next 24 hours. Mid-term means the next 30 days. Long-term represents the rest of your life. Remember, make your goals *specific, measurable, attainable, relevant,* and *timely*.

1. Short-term goals (next 24 hours)
   a. _____
   b. _____
   c. _____
   d. _____

2. Mid-term goals (next 30 days)
   a. _____
   b. _____
   c. _____
   d. _____

3. Long-term goals (rest of your life)
   a. _____
   b. _____
   c. _____
   d. _____

---

8 G.T. Doran, "There's a S.M.A.R.T. Way to Write Management Goals and Objectives," Management Review (AMA Forum), November 1981, vol. 70, no. 11, pp. 35-36.

Day 16: What Life Could Be Like

God's Word for Today

"I want you to paint it," Pope Julius II told Michelangelo Buonarroti.

The artist was stunned. He said, "This job is beyond me. Get Raphael to do it."

"Nonsense," said the Pope. "The assignment is yours."

So with one stroke of his brush, Michelangelo began the overwhelming task of painting the ceiling of the Sistine Chapel. Month after month, each day was the same. The artist worked alone, lying on a scaffold and painting the ceiling above his head. As paint dripped into his eyes, his entire body ached from the arduous work. But Michelangelo stayed at the task. Four years later, one final stroke completed the immense project.

While the final stroke was one of ecstasy, imagine the first. That first stroke seemed without purpose to the casual observer.

Only in the eyes of the great artist – who already had the painting finished in his mind – did the initial stroke mean anything.

"The secret to getting ahead is getting started."

Every journey begins with a first stroke. The strokes you paint today will shape the final picture of your life.

Mark Twain said, "The secret to getting ahead is getting started."

Moses' successor was a man named Joshua. The task of leading Israel into the Promised Land fell to him. The time for planning had ended; the time to step out had come. "So the people crossed over opposite Jericho" (Joshua 3:16).

Before Joshua could reach the Promised Land, he had to cross the Jordan River. In order to do that, he had to take the first step.

Like Michelangelo, there is a canvas in front of you. You will spend the rest of your life painting. Start with the end in mind. Now, take out your brush and get started.

Today's Exercise

Imagine a life absent from your addictive behaviors. What if there was no more porn, masturbation, adultery, affairs, massage parlors, or prostitution? What would your life be like then?

Take a few minutes and write the story of what your life would be like if you were 100% sober. Focus on four areas.

1. If I was sober, my spiritual life would be: _____
   _____
   _____
   _____

2. If I was sober, my family life would be: _____
   _____
   _____
   _____

3. If I was sober, my financial life would be: _____
   _____
   _____
   _____

4. If I was sober, my future would be: _____
   _____
   _____
   _____

Day 17: Addiction Interactive Map

God's Word for Today

I love the story of the little boy whose mother took him to the animal shelter to pick out a dog. He chose the homeliest looking puppy, but one whose tail was wagging briskly. His mom asked the boy why he picked that particular dog. The boy said, "I wanted the dog with a happy ending."

We all like happy endings.

Here's the good news. We win. For those whose faith is in their Higher Power, there is coming a day when "He will wipe every tear from their eyes. There will be no more death, no more tears, no more sorrow, and no more pain" (Revelation 21:4).

You may be in a battle today – for custody of your eyes, purity of thought, and sobriety. And while you may not win every battle, you will win the war. Your story has a happy ending.

"Starting strong is good. Finishing strong is epic."

Robin Sharma, Canadian writer and speaker, says, "Starting strong is good. Finishing strong is epic."

Billy Sunday used a baseball analogy. "Stopping at third adds no more to the score than striking out. It doesn't matter how well you start if you fail to finish."

So keep your eye on the prize. There is coming a day when you will be victorious. The road ahead will be marred by pot holes, occasional detours, and moments of discouragement. But I've read the end of the book. There is a happy ending.

Today's Exercise

Patrick Carnes offers an innovation recovery tool he calls "The Addiction Interactive Map."[9] Carnes addresses areas of stress and chaos that present dilemmas for those of us in recovery. Today, we will do a scaled back version.

If your goal is to have a happy ending, you must engage your areas of stress and chaos, and the issues which bring you down. You need to identify those areas that can bring slips or relapse.

Part of reaching your goals is dealing with the distractions that can knock you off-course. So let's go to work.

1. Stress: What are the areas of stress that you struggle with most, that make you the most vulnerable? _____
   _____
   _____

2. Chaos: Identify the craziness of your life at the moment, that can bring distraction from your goals. _____
   _____
   _____

3. Chronic issues: What are the recurring challenges you face every day? _____
   _____
   _____
   _____

---

9 Carnes, *Recovery Zone* (Carefree, AZ: Gentle Path Press, 2009), 44-45.

Day 18: Red Light, Green Light

God's Word for Today

A mailman with a new route came to a house with a mean-looking dog on the porch. When he approached the mailbox, the dog jumped 20 feet in the air, and then sat down. The owner walked out to check on the commotion.

The mailman asked in amazement, "Why did your dog do that?"

The owner replied, "We removed the chain yesterday, but he doesn't realize it yet."

Like many of us, the dog was living in the past. He assumed that yesterday's chains still had him bound today. The mailman triggered his reaction. He jumped and barked, but acted like he was still chained to his past.

Freedom from your addiction is a daily choice. Yesterday's chains do not bind you today; only today's choices can do that. Like the dog, you will be triggered sometime today. That is not a choice. But how you respond is a choice.

"Yesterday's chains do not bind you today; only today's choices can do that."

The Bible tells the story of a man bound by chains. When he was set free, for the first time in his life he was found "in his right mind" (Mark 5:15).

Sobriety does that. It puts us in our right minds. But we can only be set free by our Higher Power, Jesus Christ. Trust him to set you free. Then live in that freedom and reject the chains of the past.

Today's Exercise

Milton Magness and Marsha Means use the red light, yellow light, and green light exercise to help their clients.[10]

Red light = Stop! Quit engaging in behaviors that clearly break your sobriety and cross the lines you have drawn to provide boundaries for your addiction. Examples: viewing porn, sex with anyone other than one's spouse, visiting sexually oriented businesses.

Yellow light = Slow! These are activities that, while they do not break your sobriety, lead you down the path toward acting out. Examples: flirting, certain movies, missing 12-step meetings, searching for past acting out partners on social media.

Green light = Go! These are activities in which you need to engage to feed your recovery. Examples: attending 12-step meetings, therapy, work with one's sponsor, prayer, hobbies, family activities, sex within marriage, worship.

Now, let's get personal. Identify at least three red light, yellow light, and green light activities in your life.

1. **Red light**
    a. _____
    b. _____
    c. _____

2. **Yellow light**
    a. _____
    b. _____
    c. _____

3. **Green light**
    a. _____
    b. _____
    c. _____

---

10 Magness and Means, *Real Hope, True Freedom*, 78-85.

Day 19: Five Causes of Your Addiction

God's Word for Today

In *Chase the Kangaroo*, Charles Cos wrote, "God calls me to be faithful. The end result is in his hands, not mine."

This week, we are talking about goals. Your primary goal should not be perfection, or even sobriety. It should be faithfulness. As St. Augustine said, "Love God, then do whatever you want."

Granted, this way of thinking flies in the face of our results-driven world. We live in an age whose god is the scoreboard, bank balance, and bathroom scale. The ends don't merely justify the means; the means no longer matter.

But in God's playbook, *the game is the scoreboard*. How you play the game of life matters. Then, when the game is over, the scoreboard goes black and the players are carried off the field on the backs of angels.

> **"Your primary goal should not be perfection, or even sobriety. It should be faithfulness."**

In recovery, pay close attention to the journey. The destination will take care of itself.

Samuel said, "Only fear the Lord and serve him faithfully with all your heart. Consider what great things he has done for you" (1 Samuel 12:24).

Today, don't choose to be great, successful, or happy. Choose to be faithful, first to God, and then to your family. Live with this singular focus. "Fear the Lord with all your heart."

Today's Exercise

Tim Clinton and Mark Laaser suggest five causes of addiction: emotional, relational, physical, behavioral, and spiritual.[11] To better understand the cause of your own struggles, rate each one on a scale of 1-5, with "5" being the strongest.

1. Emotional _____

    One study found that 81 percent of sex addicts have been sexually abused, 74 percent physically abused, and 97 percent emotionally abused.

2. Relational _____

    Interpersonal relationships, from early family life to marriage, often contribute to one's addiction.

3. Physical _____

    Many addicts become physically dependent on their substance or behavior, experiencing withdrawal without them.

4. Cognitive _____

    Irrational thoughts and unrealistic expectations harm the addict's ability to cope without his or her "drug."

5. Spiritual _____

    At its core, addiction is rebellion against God. The addictive behavior becomes a false idol.

---

11 Tim Clinton and Mark Laaser, *The Quick-Reference Guide to Sexuality & Relationship Counseling* (Ada, MI: Baker Books, 2010), 151-152.

Day 20: What About Masturbation?

God's Word for Today

Larry Walker wanted to fly. It was his greatest passion and dream. Not born with wings, he had to be creative. He hitched up 45 helium-filled balloons to his lawn chair. He strapped himself in, with a snack, soft drink, and pellet gun. His plan was to rise 30 feet into the air, then shoot the balloons to bring about a slow, gentle landing.

Larry overshot his target. His lawn chair rocketed to heights of 16,000 feet! He then shot his balloons until he landed in some power lines. When arrested, he explained to the police, "A man can't just sit there."

"If all you do is what you've done, then all you'll get is what you've got."

Recovery is nothing more than redirected passion. It calls us to a universe where the impossible becomes possible, the unimaginable reality.

We really can be free! We can fly – above circumstances, temptation, and our past. But it starts with a passion to go where we have never been and do what we have not tried.

That sage philosopher Yogi Berra said it like this: "If all you do is what you've done, then all you'll get is what you've got."

And God said it like this: "The Lord said to Moses, 'Leave your country, your people, and your father's household and go to the land I will show you'" (Genesis 12:1).

God has big plans for your life. You've been grounded by your addiction long enough. Now it's time to fly.

Today's Exercise

In your goal of absolute purity, you must confront the "M" word - *masturbation*.

While this space does not allow for an extended discussion on this controversial subject, I will offer five observations and suggestions.

First, there is no universal position on the subject, even among Christian therapists. While some find all masturbation out of bounds, others "allow" for it for single adults or those whose spouses are physically incapable of fulfilling their sexual desires.

Second, sex is a desire, not a need. In SA fellowships, all masturbation is considered out of bounds for this reason. The thinking is that any sexual outlet other than with one's spouse leads down a slippery slope.

Third, masturbation is generally associated with fantasy. And this fantasy is usually connected to porn or euphoric recall. This establishes a pattern in which the addict disengages from his wife, assuming he is married.

Fourth, masturbation often becomes a substitute for "the real thing." Many spouses complain that their mate has sex with himself more than within marriage.

Fifth, ultimately, you must decide whether masturbation is acceptable within your context. This decision must be made carefully, with prayer, and in consultation with your therapist and/or sponsor.

This is your exercise. Answer the "M" question. What is your view on masturbation? Do you have a peace about including this behavior as a part of your regular lifestyle?

Yes _____
No _____

Day 21: Recovery Day

God's Word for Today

One of the most misinterpreted verses in the Bible is Matthew 22:39, "Love your neighbor as yourself," which was predicated on Jesus' first command, that you "Love the Lord your God with all your heart and with all your soul and with all your mind" (22:37).

With these two commands, Jesus narrowed the 600-plus Jewish laws emanating from the Law of Moses. A better two-point summary of the Twelve Steps cannot be found: Love God, love others.

"Sobriety was the greatest gift I ever gave myself."

But notice the part we miss. Jesus said to love others "as you love yourself." In recovery, we must connect with God and with others, but also with ourselves. The best way you can do that is to stay sober.

Rob Lowe said, "Sobriety was the greatest gift I ever gave myself." That is the gift you need to give yourself. No one else can do that for you.

Love yourself enough today to give yourself the gift of sobriety. To maintain sobriety, we must work as though it all depends on us, and then pray as though it all depends on God. Partner with him to maintain sobriety. Today, love God. Love others. But don't forget to love yourself.

We will give you an exercise that you need to repeat every month. It will be one of the best ways to secure long-term sobriety.

Today's Exercise

One of the best pieces of advice my sponsor ever gave me was to do a monthly Recovery Day. My first response was to ask, "Great! What's a Recovery Day?"

After he explained the concept to me, I embraced it. That was several years ago. I still try to do a Recovery Day once a month. It is a phenomenal tool for recovery.

A Recovery Day is a day set aside for recovery activities – all day. This provides a re-set, a fresh focus. It helps to clear the mind and re-establish the routines that brought recovery in the first place.

Your Recovery Day must be your own, customized to your needs. But generally, it should include the following: a 12-step meeting, reading recovery materials, intentionally connecting with God, meditation/reflection, setting new goals, and relaxation.

Only you can decide the specifics of your Recovery Day. It's never too soon to start planning. To get started, answer the following questions.

1. When will your first Recovery Day be?
   _____

2. In what way will you focus on recovery?
   _____

3. What will you do to connect with God?
   _____

4. What 12-step meeting will you attend?
   _____

WEEK 4

SURRENDER

"While what we call 'our own life' remains agreeable, we will not surrender it to Him."
- C. S. Lewis

Day 22: The Best Decision Ever

God's Word for Today

Five frogs sat on a log. Three decided to jump off. How many remained on the log? Answer: five. Here's the thing. Deciding to do something and actually doing it are not the same thing.

A million times, you decided to stop acting out in your addiction. But you didn't really stop. Why? Because decision and action are two different things.

Today we start week three – *surrender*. Once you accept the fact that you have a problem (week one) and become desperate to find recovery (week two), you are ready to let God do for you what you cannot do for yourself. But surrender is not passive; it requires follow-through.

"Nothing matters more to recovery than surrender."

James warned his readers, "Be doers of the Word, and not hearers only, deceiving yourselves" (James 1:22).

Addiction is all about deception. We deceive ourselves into thinking we can stop anytime, that we are really in control, and that we don't need God's help. And when we decide to stop our destructive routines, we think that this decision will be enough.

Decisions are not enough. They must be followed by action.

Zig Ziglar said, "It was character that got us out of bed, commitment that moved us into action, and discipline that enabled us to follow through."

Nothing matters more to recovery than surrender. You cannot get well until you surrender to God. And that starts with a decision – but it doesn't end there.

Make a decision – to go to meetings, pray, get a sponsor, and seek God daily. Then move from decision to action. Get off the log. It's time to jump!

Today's Exercise

According to multiple sources, the average number of decisions a person makes in a normal day is about 35,000. That includes impulsive and logic thinking, where more complex decisions are made.

That breaks down to 24 decisions per minute, including when we are asleep. I don't know how that is possible, but here's the point - we make a lot of decisions every day.

Large or medium? Black or white? Swiss or American? Hot or cold? Now or later? Exercise or sleep? One scoop or two?

But there is one decision that matters more than all others. That is the decision to turn your life and will over to the care of God. In 12-step work, it's called the Third Step Prayer, which we will memorize, starting tomorrow.

It's a simple question: Have you surrendered your addiction to God? More importantly, have you surrendered your life to God? If not, why not? And if not now, then when?

In your own words, write out a prayer of surrender to God, and then pray that prayer.

Day 23: The 3rd Step Prayer

God's Word for Today

Tourists visit the Hawaiian Island of Molokai to enjoy the beaches and charm. But Father Damien came for a different reason. He came to help people die. You see, lepers came here first, starting in about 1840. They lived in isolation, on a tract of land set aside just for them.

In 1873 Father Damien heard of their plight, so he begged his supervisors to let him move to Molokai to live with the lepers. He said, "I want to sacrifice myself for the lepers."

Damien entered the world of the lepers. He dressed their sores, hugged their children, and buried their dead. Eventually, he would contract their disease. On April 15, 1889, Father Damien died of leprosy.

> *"You have the power to overcome every temptation because of what Jesus has done."*

Father Damien did for the Molokai lepers what Jesus did for each of us. Not content to simply "treat" man, Jesus became a man. He joined the human race. The Bible says, "It was necessary for him to be made in every respect like us so that he could be our merciful and faithful High Priest before God" (Hebrews 2:17).

You have the power to overcome every temptation because of what Jesus has done. Not content to simply look down on us from above, he joined us. You are not alone. Because he became man, Christ knows exactly what you are going through, and he will walk with you every step of the way.

Recognize that you are not alone. Embrace the one who understands every temptation you will ever face – because he's been there. In fact, he still is.

Today's Exercise

I hope you are attending a 12-step group. It doesn't take long before you encounter the Third Step Prayer. Learning this prayer, and then praying this prayer are a part of working the third step. This week's theme is surrender, and that is what this prayer is all about. Many of us have made it a practice to pray this prayer every day. Commit this to memory, starting today. A good way to memorize something is by writing it. So re-write this prayer at the bottom of the page.

"God, I offer myself to you, to build with me and do with me as you will. Relieve me of the bondage of self, that I may better do your will. Take away my difficulties, that victory over them may bear witness to those I would help of your power, your love, and your way of life."

Day 24: The Addiction Cycle

God's Word for Today

Vance Havner wrote, "God uses broken things. It takes broken soil to produce a crop, broken clouds to give rain, broken grain to give bread, and broken bread to give strength. In the Gospels, it is the broken alabaster box that gives perfume. And it is Peter, weeping bitterly, who returns to greater power than ever."

God blesses brokenness. It is a key building block to recovery. When King David committed sexual sin with Bathsheba, he revealed the fallen character of man. We want what we shouldn't have and then we don't want it once we have it.

That's how it works with addiction. We crave the next drink, cigarette, drug, or encounter. That it is wrong does not matter in the moment. The key to recovery is not that we acted out – it's what comes next.

"We want what we shouldn't have, and then we don't want it once we have it."

For David, what came next was brokenness. Out of shame he found grace. David wrote, "My sacrifice, O God, is a broken and contrite heart" (Psalm 51:17).

What matters is not the size of your addiction, but the size of your brokenness. Most addicts are willing to do different things, but aren't willing to become different people. Recovery is not about bending; it's about breaking. Recovery means standing out from the crowd.

There is a saying in Narcotics Anonymous – "Every time I draw a clean breath, I'm like a fish out of water." You cannot get well until you are willing to be a fish out of water. Brokenness hurts. It doesn't come easily nor heal quickly. But it is an undeniable building block to lasting recovery.

Today's Exercise

Like King David, we want what we shouldn't have, then we don't want it once we have it. Within seconds of acting out, we feel remorse. We say, "Never again!" And we mean it. But within a few hours or days, we find ourselves back in the same place again. The process repeats itself – endlessly.

Mark Laaser has introduced what has become a standard model for this process of addiction. It is known as the *addiction cycle*.[12]

First, there is *preoccupation*. We fixate on the fantasy, image, or person. Our sexual thoughts occupy our minds nearly every hour of every day.

Second, this leads to *ritualization*. We act out in our minds what we want to do with our bodies. We play out the specific time, place, and details of what we would do if we followed through with our fantasies.

Third, *sexual compulsivity* follows next. We act on our fantasy, our ritualization. What we thought yesterday becomes what we do today.

Fourth, there is *despair*. After we act out, we feel remorse and repentance. We commit that this will never happen again.

Here's your exercise for today. Think about the last time you acted out. Think about how you went from preoccupation to ritualization to sexual compulsivity to despair.

Now, here's the key. Cut it off at the beginning. Your problem isn't really sexual compulsivity; it's preoccupation. That's the root; acting out is the predicable fruit. So start refocusing your mind to things that are pure and healthy the next time you find yourself drifting into preoccupation.

---

12 Carnes, *Out of the Shadows*, 26.

Day 25: What to Surrender

God's Word for Today

To find recovery, every addict must make a decision. Jeb Bush said, "Life teaches you that you have to make decisions in the right time – not too early and not too late." It is never too early to make the decision to confront your addiction and find recovery.

With the Egyptians hot on his trail, Moses came to the Red Sea. God's children cried out to him in desperation. Then the Lord said something strange: "Why are you crying out to me? Tell the Israelites to move on" (Exodus 14:15). In other words, make a decision to trust me and then follow through with that decision. It's all or nothing.

"There comes a time, if we hope to be overcomers, when we must take a stand and make a decision."

History tells the story of Hernán Cortez, who led 400 explorers to the new world in 1519. Stepping onto the shore of present-day Mexico, the men were prepared to split into two groups. One group would explore the land while the other would stay back to guard their 11 ships. That way, if there was a native attack, they'd have a way of escape.

But Cortez shocked his men with this command – "Burn the ships!" This cut off any possible means of escape or a return to the safety of their homeland.

Cortez made the decision you and I must make to win the battle with addiction. He went all in, no matter the cost. We have cried out to God in confession and repentance. But there comes a time, if we hope to be overcomers, when we must take a stand and make a decision. We must go all in with our recovery. There can be no Plan B. It's time to burn the ships.

Today's Exercise

Cortez burned his ships. There was no turning back. In recovery, those ships represent anything that we look to as a back-up plan. We hold onto that old phone number just in case our marriage doesn't work out. We keep that cash stashed away just in case we change our mind and return to our old habit. We keep the email address just in case we need to reconnect at some point.

"Just in case" is the enemy of recovery. You must go all in, whether your marriage survives or not, whether you keep your job or not, and whether it feels good or not.

List some ships you need to "burn." Be honest. What are those things you are holding onto "just in case"? You know you need to burn the ships. There's no better time than now.

1. _____
2. _____
3. _____
4. _____
5. _____
6. _____
7. _____
8. _____
9. _____
10. _____

Day 26: Training the Mind

God's Word for Today

On April 9, 1865, Gen. Robert E. Lee surrendered his forces to Ulysses S. Grant and the Union Army at Appomattox, Virginia. It was then, and only then, that the killing would stop, peace could find its way, and the bloodiest war in American history could come to a merciful end.

Surrender is the crux of recovery. Until you surrender your life and will to God, you will be fighting your addiction in your own strength. And that has never worked for anyone.

> *"In life we succeed because of something we did. But when we step into the arena of recovery, we discover it's about Someone Else's ideas."*

What does it mean to surrender? It involves reaching out to your Higher Power, but it is more than that. Oswald Chambers wrote, "If you have only come as far as asking God for things, you have never come to the point of understanding the least bit of what surrender really means."

Surrender is a road not easily traveled. William Ernest Henley's words have become our words.

"It matters not how strait the gate, how charged with punishments the scroll. I am the master of my fate. I am the captain of my soul."

In life we succeed because of something we did. It's about our education, our decisions, our hard work, our leadership, and our ideas. But when we step into the arena of recovery, we discover it's about Someone Else's ideas. We must surrender to the Captain of our soul.

Today's Exercise

In order to surrender our lives we must surrender our minds. That's where addiction happens – in the mind. Addicts act out what they think out. We never find victory until we learn to manage fantasy, ritualization, and euphoric recall.

Dr. Magness has made a marvelous contribution at this point. He identifies eight specific strategies for taming the mind.[13]

First, we must practice *thought replacement*. When an errant thought intrudes our minds, we learn to replace it immediately with thoughts that are wholesome.

Second, we practice the *"Double P."* We pop and pray. When we see something or someone and are triggered, we stop instantly and pray for that person and ourselves.

Third, we learn *thought stoppage*. We cut off our train of thought before it gets away from us, pulling us to the point of no return.

Fourth, we do a *feelings check*. This means we take a moment to reflect on our feelings and process our emotions.

Fifth, we engage in *prayer and meditation*. This becomes a habit, a part of our daily routine. By injecting this into our day, we build the necessary strength to withstand intrusive thoughts.

Sixth, we schedule *intrusive thoughts*. These are good thoughts. At a certain time each day, we become intentional about our focus.

Seventh, we learn the art of *reframing*. We take the intrusive thought and pivot to something else. We turn a negative into a positive.

Eighth, we make an *attitude shift*. We expect to have good thoughts. We anticipate good feelings and a spiritual presence at the start of each day.

Now, which of these practices will you adopt for today?

---

13 Magness, *Thirty Days to Hope & Freedom* (Carefree, AZ: Gentle Path Press, 2010), 109-115.

Day 27: Beyond the Crowd

God's Word for Today

Dwight L. Moody said, "Let God have your life. He can do more with it than you can." Submission to God is a precursor to sobriety. And it cannot be done in isolation. That is why God created this thing called the church.

The writer of Hebrews warned, "Do not forsake the assembling of yourselves together, as is the custom of some" (Hebrews 10:25).

God has given us two institutions: the family and the church. The church is so important that Jesus died for the church. Still, many try to maintain sobriety apart from fellowship in the church. They are playing with fire.

> *"I have never met a person who said, 'I used to attend church, but God told me to stop going.'"*

Moody knew a man in his community who had this attitude about the church. "I don't need the church to find God," he told the famous preacher.

One night, Moody paid the man a visit. Immediately, the man became defensive. "I know why you are here," he said. "But I'm telling you, I don't need the church."

Quietly, Moody walked over to the fireplace and removed one coal. Within a few minutes, that burning coal had gone cold. Message received. The man got the point. We burn brightly as long as we are with other "coals." But we go cold when trying to live the Christian life on our own.

I have never met a person who said, "I used to attend church, but God told me to stop going." Going to church has many benefits. One is that it is obedience to God. Obedience leads to submission and submission leads to sobriety.

Today's Exercise

God wants us to be as involved in church as our schedules allow. If you are in recovery, your church especially needs you. In my book, *Porn in the Pew*, I cited some alarming statistics on porn use in the church. Whereas 64 percent of men in America view porn once a month, in the church, that number is nearly the same, at 62 percent. And 37 percent of pastors struggle with porn.

You need to understand two things: you need the church and the church needs you.

There are five levels of church involvement. At which level are you today? Whichever level that is, make a commitment to move to the next level. Check your current level of involvement.

1. **Community** _____

    You attend church, but not frequently.

2. **Crowd** _____

    You attend a church, but have not joined.

3. **Congregation** _____

    You have joined a church and attend most Sundays.

4. **Committed** _____

    You are an active member of a small group.

5. **Core** _____

    You have a role in which you serve in your church.

Day 28: The 7th Step Prayer

God's Word for Today

A sign hanging on a wall in a small business read, "The 57 Rules of Success: Rule #1 – Deliver the goods. Rule #2 – The other 56 rules don't matter."

When I was a small boy, we had a milkman who "delivered the goods" right to our front door. The grocery store did the same thing. Mom never accepted excuses. They either delivered the goods or they were in real trouble.

Jesus "delivered the goods" like no one before or after. But he kept things pretty simple. While the religious crowd was all about rules, Jesus had just one for his earliest followers. "Come, follow me" (Matthew 4:19).

> *"While the religious crowd was all about rules, Jesus had just one – 'Come, follow me.'"*

Sure, other rules would follow – rules about how to love God and others, rules about how to care for the hurting and minister to the poor. But it was Rule #1 that served as a foundation for all the others. "Come, follow me."

The Christian life is not about rules. It's about relationship. And that's good news for those of us with hurts, habits, and hang-ups. Jesus didn't tell Peter, James, and John to figure it all out and then follow him. Why? Because we can't figure it out until we follow him.

That takes us back to this week's theme again – surrender. How can you explain why 12 men would walk away from their jobs, homes, and security in order to follow a man they had just met? It made no sense. But they knew it was right.

Rule #1 – Follow Jesus.

Today's Exercise

Jesus had one overarching rule – "Come, follow me." Nothing he ever said called for surrender more than that first commandment. As we complete the fourth week, you need to nail that down – surrender. Why? Because until you are surrendered to God completely you cannot tap into his power. And without his power, you are helpless and hopeless in your battle for sanity and recovery.

If you are working the 12 steps, this next prayer will be familiar to you. The seventh step is all about total surrender – holding nothing back. As you did with the Third Step Prayer, read it, then write it below.

> "My Creator, I am now willing that you should have all of me, good and bad. I pray that you now remove from me every single defect of character which stands in the way of my usefulness to you and my fellows. Grant me strength, as I go out from here, to do your bidding."

WEEK 5

DISCIPLINES

"Winners embrace hard work. They love the discipline of it, the trade-off they're making to win. Losers, on the other hand, see it as punishment. And that's the difference."
- Lou Holtz

Day 29: Get in the Word

God's Word for Today

Mark Twain said, "You can't depend on your eyes when your imagination is out of focus." Addiction is at its roots a battle of the imagination. From sinister imaginations come sinister acting out. Until our minds come into focus, sobriety will be a mirage.

Your mind cannot get into focus if you are looking in the wrong direction. To have a better future, you have to quit trying to have a better past.

This week, we are learning seven disciplines that are integral to lasting recovery. The first is our need to be in God's Word every day. Nothing will do more to capture your focus and build a foundation for recovery.

"To have a better future, you have to quit trying to have a better past."

Paul told young Timothy as much. "Study to show yourself approved, a workman who needs not be ashamed, rightly dividing the Word of truth" (2 Timothy 2:15).

To be a good workman we must acquire the right tools. God's Word is the first tool in our tool box. That's why we read our Bibles every day. It brings life – and recovery – into focus.

Alexander Graham Bell offered this analogy. "Consecrate your thoughts upon the work at hand. The sun's rays do not burn until brought to a focus."

God's Word brings everything into focus.

Today's Exercise

There's no such thing as a bad Bible. But we recommend the best Bible – for recovery. It's called the Life Recovery Bible. Published in 1998, this unique study Bible was put together by 24 editors and 27 writers, and it contains hundreds of devotions and amazing insight on recovery. Contact our ministry, and we will ship you a copy of the Life Recovery Bible at no cost to you.

It is good to read the Word every day, but better to apply it. Try the "SOAP" method. Take a moment right now to read the story of the Prodigal Son, found in Luke 15:11-32. Then fill in the blanks.

1. Scripture

    One or two verses that really spoke to you: _____
    _____

2. Observations

    Two or three things you observed from this passage: _____
    _____

3. Application

    How does this apply to your life? _____
    _____

4. Prayer

    Write out a prayer based on this passage: _____
    _____
    _____

Day 30: Pray – Here's How

God's Word for Today

There is a simple reason that prayer is a key building block to recovery. Oswald Chambers said it like this: "It's not so much that prayer changes things, but that prayer changes me."

Prayer is about connecting with our Higher Power. Gandhi said, "Prayer is not asking. It is a longing of the soul. In prayer, it is better to have a heart without words than words without heart." Recovery prayer is not an outcome-based prayer. It's about making a spiritual connection.

C.S. Lewis prayed for the healing of his wife, who was near death. When she recovered for a time, a friend told the great philosopher, "God answered your prayers! You prayed for your wife's recovery and God answered!"

"It's not so much that prayer changes things, but that prayer changes me."

Lewis responded, "I did not pray because my wife was sick. I prayed because I can't help it. The power of prayer is not that it changes my circumstances, but that it changes my heart."

One day, Jesus' disciples made an unusual request. "Lord, teach us to pray" (Luke 11:1). Notice, they did not ask Jesus to teach them how to pray, but to simply *pray*.

In today's exercise, I will give you a simple formula for how to pray. But what matters most is not how you pray or what you pray – but that you pray. Make the disciples' request your request today. "Lord, teach us to pray!"

Today's Exercise

Let me teach you a formula that I learned decades ago. It is simple, but it works. Most of us need something to keep our prayers on track; this plan will do that.

Think of "ACTS," as in the Book of the Bible. Each letter stands for one-fourth of your daily prayer. Set aside a few minutes to pray. Write down a few specifics below.

1. **Adoration**

   Tell God something you adore about him. Write it below.
   _____
   _____

2. **Confession**

   Confess a sin to God. Write that sin here: _____
   _____

3. **Thanksgiving**

   Thank God for something specific in your life: _____
   _____

4. **Supplication**

   Ask God for something specific: _____
   _____
   _____

Day 31: The Magic of 12 Steps

God's Word for Today

Paul wrote, "No temptation has taken you except what is common to man. And God is faithful; he will not let you be tempted beyond what you can bear. But when you are tempted, he will also provide a way out so that you can endure it" (1 Corinthians 10:13).

So what is that "way out" for the addict? I suggest you try what I was afraid to try. Go to meetings. Yes, go to 12-step meetings.

If you resist going to meetings, I respond in two ways. First, I was there myself. I fought the idea for years. But now, 500 meetings later, I can tell you going to 12-step meetings was one of my best decisions ever. In fact, I still go – twice a week.

> *"Not joining a 12-step group has you in the mess you're in."*

Second, how's your current plan working for you? I'm guessing the reason you have this workbook is not that you couldn't find anything else to read. I'm guessing you have a problem. And I'm guessing that trying to fix it on your own isn't working too well. It rarely does.

Alan Lakein famously said, "Failing to plan is planning to fail." One study showed that the chances of recovery without a comprehensive plan is one in 10,000.

Recovery is hard work. Twelve-step work is not easy. Not joining a 12-step group has you in the mess you're in. I suggest it's time to try something else.

This may offend you, but I'm going to say it anyway. Millions of us have found years of absolute sobriety through 12-step work. You have not.

Today's Exercise

Few find recovery apart from a group. A 12-step group provides the kind of encouragement, written materials, and fellowship that facilitate recovery. Take these three steps toward recovery today.

1. **Find a group.**

    There are many 12-step groups available. You can probably find a group in your area. Phone meetings are also an option. For your first year of recovery, you should try to attend two meetings per week. These are three options:

    a. Sexaholics Anonymous (sa.org)
    b. Sex Addicts Anonymous (saa-recovery.org)
    c. Celebrate Recovery (celebraterecovery.com)

2. **Get a sponsor.**

    When you begin attending meetings, you will hear about sponsors. These are men or women (choose someone of your own sex) who guide others through the 12-step process. Within a month of attending meetings, you should find a sponsor.

3. **Work the steps.**

    There is a phrase you will hear in meetings: "It works if you work it." The 12 steps follow a biblical model for recovery and restoration. Begin working the steps with the help of your sponsor.

Day 32: I Confess

God's Word for Today

We used to have a Cocker Spaniel named Duffy. She was one happy mess. Her bladder was unable to control her joy. We were always cleaning up after her. She slobbered horribly. When she'd run or shake her head, slobber went everywhere. And what she messed up, we cleaned up.

One day, due to a back problem that is common to Cockers, Duffy became paralyzed. She couldn't walk or get to her food dish. We spent a king's ransom on her back surgery, knowing it might not be successful. Then we had to wait and see. We fed her by hand and carried her outside where she could at least enjoy the view.

> **"God loves you more than he hates your mess."**

It took a few weeks, but eventually, she began to move again and she fully recovered. But she was still a mess. So why did we continue to clean up after her, no matter how bad it got? It's simple. We loved our dog more than we hated her mess.

You are a mess. But know this. God loves you more than he hates your mess.

And that brings us to today's discipline. We must confess our mess – our sins. And when we do, we have this guarantee from God: "Their sins and lawless acts will I remember no more" (Hebrews 10:17).

A.W. Tozer said, "You have been forgiven, so act like it!" Confess your addiction, slip, or relapse to God. When we confess our sins, God cleanses us (1 John 1:9). Why? Because he is in the mess-cleaning business. And he loves you more than he hates your mess.

Today's Exercise

Here's a strange exercise for you to try. Sorry, but this is for guys only – and any women with beards. This comes from George N. Collins, author of *Breaking the Cycle*.[14] Collins suggests that every time you objectify a woman or feel tempted, you should run your open palm across your cheek, moving from your jawline up (against the direction facial hair grows). If you feel hair, let that be a reminder that you are a man.

You don't have to give into your sexual appetite any more than you are a slave to other behaviors in which you indulged as a child or adolescent.

The intrusive thoughts will still come from time to time. Don't beat yourself up over that. But the next time you are tempted, try the beard test. Remind yourself of what Paul said. You are no longer bound by the appetites of your past (1 Corinthians 13:11).

---

14 George N. Collins, *Breaking the Cycle: Free Yourself from Sex Addiction* (Oakland, CA: New Harbinger Publications, 2011), 64.

Day 33: Once-a-Week

God's Word for Today

Oswald Chambers said, "The greatest competitor of devotion to Jesus is service for him."

God created human beings, not human doings. God is far more concerned with what is going on in you than what is going on around you. And what he is looking for is not production as much as passion.

I love the way John Piper puts it. "One of the greatest uses of Twitter and Facebook will be to prove at the Last Day that prayerlessness was not from lack of time."

In overcoming our addictions, it is critical that we discover a passion for God. And one of the best ways to do that is to engage in worship once a week. It is so important, in fact, that the Bible says to "not forsake the assembling of yourselves together, as is the custom of some" (Hebrews 10:25).

> *"Perhaps you have been hurt by the local church. The answer is not to abandon the church. The answer is to find a new church."*

Perhaps you have been hurt by the local church. The answer is not to abandon the church – the body of Christ. The answer is to find a new church.

Weekly worship is a necessary discipline for recovery. From the Ten Commandments (honor the Sabbath) to the New Testament Church (which met weekly on The Lord's Day), the importance of weekly worship is clear.

You were created for the body of Christ. And the body of Christ was created for you.

Today's Exercise

I encourage you to do two things. First, find a church, if you don't already have one. Prioritize the following list of things to look for in a church, then commit to visiting at least three churches in your area over the next few weeks. Prayerfully select a church based on these priorities. List, from 1 to 10, the order of what matters most to you in a local church.

_____ Preaching
_____ Music
_____ Children's ministry
_____ Student ministry
_____ Proximity to your home
_____ Small groups
_____ Doctrine
_____ Denomination
_____ Personal relationships
_____ Opportunities to serve

Second, try the 1-1-1 Plan. By that, I mean that you commit three hours a week to your church. As with recovery, when it comes to church, the measure you give will be the measure you get back. Don't go to church just for you. Give one hour a week to each of the following:

1. Worship
2. Small group
3. Service

Day 34: Shape Up!

God's Word for Today

A few years ago, Pastor Rick Warren confessed to his church that he had not taken proper care of his body, as he was 25 pounds overweight. That led to the popular *Daniel Plan,* which begins with these words: "Everything God makes has a purpose." That includes your body.

Often, when an addict turns from his chemical, substance, or habit, he turns to another chemical, substance, or habit. By one estimate, two-thirds of sex addicts are also overweight. They fail to see the relevance of taking care of their bodies.

God says three things about your body.

First, your body belongs to God. "The body is not meant for sexual immorality, but for the Lord, and the Lord for the body" (1 Corinthians 6:13).

"Jesus paid for your body when he died on the cross."

Second, Jesus paid for your body when he died on the cross. Paul wrote, "You are the temple of the Holy Spirit. You are not your own. You were bought with a price" (1 Corinthians 6:19-20).

Third, God expects you to take care of your body. It is his gift to you. What you do with it is your gift to him. Everything about you matters to God – including your weight, conditioning, and overall physical health.

Jesus said, "Love the Lord with all your strength" (Luke 10:27). Don't compartmentalize life into the spiritual, intellectual, emotional, and physical. It all matters to God.

Today's Exercise

You have a plan for most areas of your life – your daily schedule, finances, marriage, children, vacations, career, retirement, and where you're going to eat lunch tomorrow. And each of those activities will require the use of the one thing you may not have a plan for – your body. Because your body matters to God, you need a plan for how to take care of your body. Take just a few minutes to list one thing you can do to take better care of your body in each of these areas. Because we are total beings, what you do with your body will affect your recovery. So take this seriously!

1. Diet: _____
2. Exercise: _____
3. Rest: _____
4. Hobby: _____
5. Lifestyle change: _____
6. Stop this: _____
7. Start this: _____

Day 35: The 20-Minute Rule

God's Word for Today

Marcus Aurelius said, "The happiness of your life depends upon the quality of your thoughts; therefore, guard accordingly, and take care that you entertain no notions unsuitable to virtue and reasonable nature."

Thoughts lead to acts, which lead to habits, which lead to character, which leads to destiny. It all starts in the head.

Many addicts put too much stock in how they *act*, as opposed to how they *think*. Sobriety is not the absence of acting out; it is progressive victory over lust. And you can lust a thousand times a day and never act out again. But Jesus said that when we lust after someone, we have already crossed the line.

> **"Recovery is more about what you do with your head than what you do with your body."**

So what is the answer? It is found in one of Jesus' last teachings. "Watch and pray so that you will not fall into temptation. The spirit is willing, but the flesh is weak" (Matthew 26:41).

Whatever your triggers may be, the dual response is the same: watch and pray. First, be on the *watch* for temptation and intrusive thoughts. Second, when an image catches your eye or a fantasy invades your thoughts, do the "double p" – *pop and pray*.

One of the most important disciplines in maintaining your sobriety will be to "take captive every thought" (2 Corinthians 10:5). Why? Because recovery is more about what you do with your head than what you do with your body.

Today's Exercise

Your exercise for today is one I can almost guarantee will serve you well for the rest of your life. This is a simple step you can take that will preserve your sobriety like nothing else. Clients tell me this is one of the best tips I've given them.

I call it the "20-minute rule." This is how it works. First, understand the premise.

For most addicts, when the urge hits to act out, the intensity will only last for 15-20 minutes. After about 20 minutes, it will pass. We will either act out or stay strong. In either case, the urge will be gone (or greatly reduced) in 20 minutes.

So you have two choices – shame and guilt or hope and freedom. And I've yet to hear from the person who said they preferred shame and guilt.

I never acted out, then later thought, "Well, that was a good idea." On the other hand, there was always regret. Always.

So, the next time you feel a great temptation coming on, remember that in 20 minutes, it will pass. You don't need to stay sober one day at a time. You only need to stay sober for about 20 minutes. So try the "20-minute rule." When temptation strikes, take the next 20 minutes to pray, call your sponsor, go for a quick run, or do anything else that is healthy.

In 20 minutes, your urge will end. But your sobriety doesn't need to.

WEEK 6

HONESTY

"No legacy is so rich as honesty."
— **William Shakespeare**

Day 36: Getting Honest

God's Word for Today

Mahatma Gandhi said, "To believe in something and not live it is dishonest." Addicts are experts on the double life. We compartmentalize. Most addicts live within a strict moral code – 99 percent of the time. But this double life eventually catches up with us.

The Bible says, "A person with divided loyalty is as unsettled as a wave of the sea that is blown and tossed by the wind" (James 1:8).

The answer is honesty. Dr. Paul Hokemeyer, Director of the Maryland Addiction Recovery Center, writes, "Complete honesty and transparency with others are key to sustainable recovery because they are key to personal and spiritual growth."

"Recovery is built on the foundation of total honesty. Nothing less will do."

Half-truths are total lies. Albert Einstein was right when he said, "Whoever is careless with the truth in small matters cannot be trusted with important matters." Recovery is built on the foundation of total honesty. Nothing less will do.

How does this work? First, you must be honest with yourself. Admit your powerlessness over your disease. Then be honest with God. Tell him what he already knows – in detail. Finally, you must be honest with a group. In many ways, a 12-step group can become your family. It's where you can be real and honest.

Those who have given themselves to God face new temptations and decisions every day. The answer is honesty – with yourself, God, and others.

Today's Exercise

Your exercises this week will have to do with facing your addiction head on – with total honesty. We will start with a two-part exercise that will be difficult, but necessary.

1. Your bottom line behaviors: list your "bottom line" behaviors – the activities you have engaged in as an addict. Do not list names or places, just the kind of activities you have sought to fulfill your sexual fantasies.

    a. _____
    b. _____
    c. _____
    d. _____

2. What your addiction has cost you: be as thorough as possible, identifying the cost over the entire time of your addiction.

    a. Relationships: _____
    _____
    _____

    b. Money: _____
    c. Career: _____
    d. Reputation: _____
    _____

    e. Time: _____

Day 37: Taking Inventory

God's Word for Today

Angelina Jolie said, "I don't see myself as beautiful, because I see a lot of flaws."

How do you see yourself? The old prophet wisely advised, "Now this is what the Lord Almighty says: 'Give careful thought to your ways'" (Haggai 1:5).

On the road to recovery, you must avoid two ditches. On one side of the road is the "I'm okay" ditch. We drive into this ditch when we refuse to acknowledge our struggles.

On the other side of the road is the "I'm a horrible human being" ditch. We drive into this ditch when we define ourselves by our shortcomings.

> *"We cannot define ourselves by our faults, nor must we run from them. Instead, we must grow from them."*

Haggai recommended driving in the middle lane. Step 4 of all 12-step programs says it like this: "We made a searching and fearless moral inventory of ourselves."

When was the last time you did that? Recovery calls for frequent take-home exams. It calls on us to take periodic moral inventories. We cannot define ourselves by our faults, nor must we run from them. Instead, we must grow from them.

Today, you will take an honest, fearless, moral inventory of yourself. Don't define yourself by your faults and don't ignore them. Acknowledge them. Confess them. Then prepare to move on.

Today's Exercise

In working Step 4 with one's sponsor, the addict confronts his defects, resentments, and fears. It is not a short process, nor is it an easy step to complete. Obviously, we cannot expect you to take a complete "fearless, moral inventory" in one brief exercise. So don't confuse this with that.

But in a sense, we need to always be working our 4th Step. We need to consistently take an honest inventory of ourselves. So take a few minutes to simply list your ten most prominent character defects.

1. _____
2. _____
3. _____
4. _____
5. _____
6. _____
7. _____
8. _____
9. _____
10. _____

Now, take a moment to pray and ask God to begin removing all of these defects of character. If you find it helpful, pray the 3rd Step Prayer: *"God, I offer myself to you, to build with me and do with me as you will. Take away my difficulties, that victory over them may bear witness to those I would help of your power, your love, and your way of life."*

Day 38: Family History

God's Word for Today

Family history is at the root of your struggles. It always is. And for those who read the Scriptures, this should not be a surprise. The Bible says, "The Lord is slow to anger, abounding in love and forgiving sin and rebellion. Yet he does not leave the guilty unpunished; he punishes the children for the sin of the parents to the third and fourth generation" (Numbers 14:18).

Mark Twain said that he had spent a large sum of money to trace his family tree. Then he spent twice as much trying to keep his ancestry a secret.

The fact is, you are a product of your parents and of their parents. Family secrets, intimacy issues, and sexuality form each of us – for better or worse, and usually some of each.

But at the end of the day, you cannot blame your family for your own mistakes. Sure, the mistakes they made and the way you were raised have contributed to your disease. But your parents never made you view porn, masturbate, or have an affair.

"You are a product of your parents and of their parents."

We will all stand before God one day. And we will stand alone, apart from our family, our friends, and the kid who picked on us on the school playground.

Paul wrote, "We must all appear before the judgment seat of Christ, so that each of us may receive what is due for the things done while in the body, whether good or bad" (2 Corinthians 5:10).

To find lasting recovery, you need to understand your family history. But it is just that – history. You can't live in the past and you can't change it. So learn from it – then move on.

Today's Exercise

It is important to understand the impact of your family history on your personal struggles with porn and sexual addiction. Below, list up to five key family members and the things they did or the way they acted that have affected your sexuality in some way. Examples may include their own sex addictions, intimacy issues, lack of affection, secrecy, or other messages they may have sent you about sex.

1. _____
   _____
   _____
   _____

2. _____
   _____
   _____
   _____

3. _____
   _____
   _____
   _____

4. _____
   _____
   _____
   _____

5. _____
   _____
   _____
   _____

Day 39: Secrets

God's Word for Today

There is a story about a man named Achan. He cost Israel 36 lives and a huge upset loss to the tiny army of Ai. Israel had just defeated mighty Jericho. But they soon learned that yesterday's success is no guarantee of tomorrow's victory. They became overconfident and they lost. Worse yet, Achan broke God's command by keeping a few valuables from the previous battle. He confessed, "I coveted the silver and gold and buried them under my tent" (Joshua 7:21).

"Man is not what he thinks he is. He is what he hides."

What Achan buried became his undoing. It would cost him his life.

The danger of our secrets is that they are our secrets. French novelist Andre Malraux wrote, "Man is not what he thinks he is; he is what he hides."

Patrick Kennedy, himself an addict, says, "No one is immune to addiction; it affects people of all ages, races, classes, and professions."

If anyone should have been immune to addiction, it would have been Patrick Kennedy. But what he saw alcohol do to so many others in his family, it would also do to him. And he did not find sobriety until he exposed his struggle to those around him. It was when he got honest and brought his secrets to the light that he got well.

It is critical to get your secrets out. In 12-step work, this is called "working the First Step." It's about letting go of your secrets. Why? Because secrets kill.

Today's Exercise

Secrets kill. Secrets are the enemy of recovery. What you hide is who you really are. Getting your secrets out will be one of the most difficult - but important - exercises in your early recovery work. It is a two-step process. First, you must come clean to yourself. And then you must come clean with one other person. So take a few minutes and write out your #1 secret - that which nobody knows. Then, in Part B of this exercise, write out the name of at least one person (and up to three) with whom you will share your secret.

Part A - Identify your secret

_____
_____
_____
_____
_____
_____
_____
_____
_____
_____

Part B - Up to three people you will tell

Name: _____
Name: _____
Name: _____

Day 40: Inner Circle

God's Word for Today

In the blink of an eye the world's strongest man threw it all away.

"Samson said to Delilah, 'A razor has never come upon my head, for I have been a Nazarite to God from my mother's womb. If my head is shaved, then my strength will leave me, and I shall become weak and be like any other man'" (Judges 16:17).

Today, we introduce the "three circles." The inner circle consists of those activities which cost us our sobriety. For Samson, that was Delilah. Samson's enemies paid her to discover the secret of his amazing strength.

> *"You need a battle plan in place before it is needed."*

Delilah was Samson's blind spot. He resisted her advances three times, but he was still playing with fire.

The inevitable happened. Samson eventually caved in to Delilah's advances. By not surrendering to God he remained blind to the danger of the foreign woman.

It didn't have to end this way. If Samson had decided what to do before the temptation hit, he would have survived. That's how it is in life. That's why you need a battle plan to be firmly in place *before it is needed*. The world is full of Delilahs, whose conniving ways may cost you everything. They come in many forms. Delilah represents the loss of sobriety. For the sake of today's lesson, Delilah represents the inner circle.

Today's Exercise

The "three circles" are a part of recovery work in the Sex Addicts Anonymous (SAA) program. Here's how it works. Take a sheet of paper and draw a large circle, with a second circle inside of that circle, and then a third, smaller circle, in the middle. We'll get to the outer circle and middle circle the next two days. For today, we will focus on the inner circle. It represents those behaviors which break our sobriety. There is no settled list; you have to decide what, for you, breaks your sobriety.

Typically, activities such as sex with anyone other than one's spouse are in the inner circle. I suggest placing masturbation and all forms of pornography here, as well. Then add those things which God has convicted you about specifically. This will be your list of inner circle behaviors. You may only have a few, or your list may be longer.

1. _____

2. _____

3. _____

4. _____

5. _____

6. _____

7. _____

Day 41: Middle Circle

God's Word for Today

If ever there was a story of a rousing accomplishment, it is the story of the world's first great ship builder. His name was Noah. Talk about crazy success! He built a huge ship, rescued a zillion animals, lived in that ship for over a year, and lived to be 950 years old.

That's not a bad life. But unfortunately, there is more to his story.

One night, Noah became intoxicated. "When he drank more wine, he became drunk and lay uncovered inside his tent. Ham, the father of Canaan, saw his father naked" (Genesis 9:21-22).

That's not an image any son should have to endure. Walking in on your naked, 900-year-old dad creates issues far beyond my level of training.

"Lot cast his tent toward Sodom, and then it was over."

The lesson of Noah is a simple one. Noah never intended to lay naked before his son. And when he started to drink, I'm sure he never intended to become completely intoxicated. But one drink led to another, and the night ended badly.

The same Book of Genesis tells us of the day Lot "cast his tent toward Sodom" (13:12). And then it was over. He never intended to move to the wicked city of Sodom; he only wanted to observe it from the hillside.

Noah and Lot both entered into middle circle behaviors. There wasn't anything wrong with Noah taking a few drinks or Lot setting up his tent on the hill outside of Sodom. The problem was that they both put themselves at risk.

As sex addicts, we do the same thing when we watch certain movies, browse certain Internet sites, and look up dating services. They are dangerous, for they put our sobriety at risk.

Today's Exercise

Today's work is a little harder than what you did yesterday. The inner circle behaviors – which break your sobriety – are pretty easy to identify. And tomorrow's outer circle behaviors will be obvious, as well. But the most important circle may be this one. Why? Because it is the middle circle behaviors that put your sobriety at risk. And the list is varied, from one person to another.

Make a list of those people, places, or predicaments which put you at risk. For some, this list includes certain parts of town, outdoor places such as amusement parks or the beach, the mall, certain magazines, etc. The list is always evolving.

1. **People**
    a. _____
    b. _____
    c. _____
    d. _____

2. **Places**
    a. _____
    b. _____
    c. _____
    d. _____

3. **Predicaments**
    a. _____
    b. _____
    c. _____
    d. _____

Day 42: Outer Circle

God's Word for Today

Revelation 2:10 says, "Do not be afraid of what you are about to suffer. I tell you, the devil will put some of you in prison to test you, and you will suffer persecution for ten days. Be faithful, even to the point of death, and I will give you life as your victor's crown."

Paul wrote, "Do not be weary in well doing" (Galatians 6:9).

Nothing is more important to recovery than to keep doing what you know to do – over and over again. It's called persistence.

In that iconic movie, *Finding Nemo*, Dory explained the key to success. "Just keep swimming. Just keep swimming. Just keep swimming, swimming, swimming. What do we do? We swim, swim, swim."

The lesson of Nemo is follow through. It's all about doing the right things over and over.

"Those who fail in recovery do so, not for lack of knowledge, but for lack of following through."

In my experience, the vast majority of those who fail in recovery do so, not for lack of knowledge, but for lack of following through with the basic habits they know they need to establish. Success in life – and recovery – is all about persistence.

Today, we conclude our week focused on honesty, and our work with the three circles. Your outer circle behaviors are those to which you need to commit, over and over, day after day.

It's one thing to know what to do. But it's a far better thing to do what you know.

Today's Exercise

For our final exercise of the week, you will identify your outer circle behaviors. These are healthy activities that make you a better person. They bring greater connection with God, balance of life, and sober living. The outer circle list can be almost endless, so we will leave plenty of space for you to work with. Consider the following examples: prayer, recovery groups, date night with your spouse, exercise, healthy diet, meditation, Scripture reading, recreational activities, walks in the park, Sunday worship, family time.

Let's get started.

1. _____
2. _____
3. _____
4. _____
5. _____
6. _____
7. _____
8. _____
9. _____
10. _____
11. _____
12. _____
13. _____
14. _____
15. _____
16. _____
17. _____
18. _____
19. _____
20. _____

WEEK 7

COMMUNITY

"Only a life lived for others is a life worthwhile."
— **Albert Einstein**

"We've been given the covenant community because we need each other, and together we'll be more mature, experience more life, and know more joy than we ever would apart from one another."
— **Matt Chandler**

Day 43: Reconnect

God's Word for Today

You can't sustain recovery on your own. Almost nobody does. You need community. You were created that way. This week, we will consider seven aspects to community.

We will begin with the most important connection – you and God. Jesus knew how critical it was to stay connected with his Father. The Bible says that he made a point of connecting with the Father in a mountain before sunrise (Mark 1:35).

One of the hardest things for any of us to believe is that we can be both fully known and truly loved – at the same time. Tim Keller writes, "To be loved but not known is comforting, but superficial. To be known and not loved is our greatest fear. To be fully known and truly loved is the greatest gift of all."

> **"To be fully known and truly loved is the greatest gift of all."**

Community starts with you and God. That's what the prophet Micah said hundreds of years before Christ. He pled for God's people in the midst of their sins. Hearing of their pending doom, Micah said, "Because of this I will weep and wail; I will go about barefoot and naked. I will howl like a jackal and moan like an owl" (Micah 1:8).

Did you catch that phrase, "barefoot and naked"? Micah was saying, "I'm desperate for God and I want to see him work. I stand empty without him."

Community begins when we come before God "barefoot and naked." When we come to him void of anything but desire to know him, we discover what it means to be both fully known and truly loved.

Today's Exercise

You will recall that on Day 21, we introduced the idea of a Recovery Day. This is something you should do once a month. But we also need other times to set aside an hour or two to reconnect with God specifically, in a focused way. Make recovery a part of that connection.

Below, I have listed a few examples of ways in which you can do this. Circle at least three activities that will help you re-engage with God and your recovery.

- Attend a 12-step meeting.
- Get away for a concentrated time of prayer.
- Do something outside (beach, lake, park).
- Have lunch with someone else in recovery.
- Read recovery literature.
- Take time for meditation.
- Read Scripture and pray.
- Set goals for your recovery.
- Do some journaling.

Now, set a day to follow through with these activities. Make it your special day.

- Date for my Recovery Day: _____

Day 44: You Need this Guy

God's Word for Today

Edmund Hillary, the first man to scale Mount Everest in 1953, said, "It is not the mountain we conquer, but ourselves."

The greatest mountain you may ever climb is Mount Recovery. And Hillary is right. The challenge is not the mountain; the challenge is you.

One day, Jesus climbed a mountain. "Jesus took with him Peter, James, and John, the brother of James, and led them up a high mountain by themselves" (Matthew 17:1).

From this simple verse we learn quite a bit about climbing mountains. We learn that we cannot do it alone. We've all heard of Edmund Hillary. But you may have never heard the name, Tenzing Norgay. Mr. Norgay was Hillary's climbing partner.

"If you are to scale Mount Recovery, you'll need others along this journey."

Even Jesus didn't climb the mountain by himself. If you are to scale Mount Recovery, you'll need others along this journey.

Every climber has a leader. Jesus didn't say, "There it is, boys, get after it!" He led them. In recovery, we need the help of experienced climbers. You need a mentor, someone who knows the way to the top.

This person may be your sponsor. Or he could be a treasured friend. He needs to be someone who will hold you accountable and ask you the tough questions. You must not climb alone.

Mount Recovery is right in front of you. It's a tall climb, one whose end is beyond what you can see from here. But with the right guide and support, it can be the most important climb of your life. But you cannot climb alone.

Today's Exercise

Consider having an accountability partner. This way you won't have to climb Mount Recovery alone. You will have a climbing partner, someone who understands you, along the journey.

Just as Edmund Hillary had Tenzing Norgay, David had Jonathan and Paul had Timothy. There are times when you need to focus on time alone with God, such as on Recovery Day. But there are also times when you need someone to talk to – someone to hold you accountable.

This person may be your sponsor. He might be a close friend. He must be someone of the same sex. And he needs to know your situation and be willing to ask the tough questions.

Write down three names of possible climbing partners. Then begin to pray and seek God's leadership as you narrow the list to one.

1. _____

2. _____

3. _____

Day 45: Three Musketeers

God's Word for Today

John Dickerson, a Founding Father of the United States, spoke to the events of his day with the famous words, "United we stand, divided we fall." These words were published in the Boston Gazette in July, 1768.

French author Alexandre Dumas picked up on this theme in writing his most famous novel, *The Three Musketeers*, in 1844. The book recants the adventures of a young man named Charles de Batz de Castelmore d'Artagnan, who left home to serve Louis XIV as captain of the Musketeers from 1632 to 1673. In a pact to remain loyal to one another through thick and thin, d'Artagnan and his fellow Musketeers adopted the following as their motto for life:

> *"None of us is as strong as all of us."*

"*All for one and one for all*; united we stand, divided we fall."

The three Musketeers might have been the first recovery group. This kind of unity and mutual support is critical to lasting sobriety and daily victory.

John Maxwell is right when he cites a key aspect to effective leadership: "None of us is as strong as all of us."

Paul said it like this: "I appeal to you, brothers and sisters, in the name of our Lord Jesus Christ, that all of you agree with one another in what you say and that there be no divisions among you, but that you be perfectly united in mind and thought" (1 Corinthians 1:10).

The road to recovery is long and winding, with many hills and valleys, passing through treacherous lands unseen until they are conquered. It is foolish to tread such a road by yourself. You need others to join you for the walk.

Say it with me: "*All for one and one for all; united we stand, divided we fall.*"

Today's Exercise

You need an inner circle. Notice what Jesus did. He spent all night in prayer before he chose the 12 disciples. Then he gave even more thought to picking the three men, from among that group, who would be his closest confidants. Then Jesus spent more time with Peter, James, and John than the other nine combined.

It is not critical that your number be three. It might be four or five. But don't rush into this. Having a small accountability group is too important to pick the wrong people.

There are several ways to go about forming this group. You might find them from among a small Bible study group. You might discover some guys in your SA or SAA group, who have similar goals for their recovery.

Your inner circle should meet once a month. These need to be men or women you can trust with your most intimate struggles. Then, "as iron sharpens iron," you will sharpen one another.

List the names of some men (or women if you are a female) you can begin to pray about being in your inner circle of accountability.

1. _____

2. _____

3. _____

4. _____

5. _____

6. _____

7. _____

Day 46: A Small Group

God's Word for Today

He was the world's most famous recluse, the hermit's hermit, and the richest man alive. His name was Howard Hughes. An aviator, industrialist, and film producer, Hughes began showing signs of mental illness while in his 30s. On Thanksgiving Day of 1966, he moved into a suite at Las Vegas' Desert Inn. He refused to leave his room. When they insisted, he bought the hotel. Howard Hughes never found the peace that comes from healthy relationships. Fittingly, ten years later, he died alone.

> *"The best way to find yourself is to lose yourself in service to others."*

We were never intended to do life alone. Few find recovery on their own. Gandhi said, "The best way to find yourself is to lose yourself in service to others." The man who stands alone will surely fall.

An elderly lady stood in line at the post office once a week, to buy stamps. The line often took about 30 minutes. An employee noted this pattern and approached the woman one day. "You do know you can buy your stamps from the stamp machine, don't you?" he asked. "Why do you stand in line for 30 minutes when you could get them so much quicker?"

The lady replied, "It's simple. When I get to the counter, the young man working there speaks to me. And he knows my name. But that stupid stamp machine never says a word."

We need others in order to win the race of life. That's why Solomon wrote, "Though one may be overpowered, two can defend themselves. A cord of three strands is not quickly broken" (Ecclesiastes 4:12).

Today's Exercise

I heard someone say, "People are not looking for a church these days. They are looking for *the* church." What they meant was that connection is not relegated to a building with a steeple on top (though we will talk about that tomorrow). People are looking for a real connection with a small group.

In my younger days, we called this "Sunday school." Today, the term "Sunday school" has been largely replaced with something like "life group." But regardless of what you call it, it still works.

Jesus set the example for us. As we have seen already this week, Jesus maintained his connection with the Father and with an inner circle. But he also had his twelve – the disciples with whom he shared his life. So important was this group to Jesus that he spent far more time with them than he did preaching to large crowds. He understood the magic of a small group.

You can find them all over. Some meet as Bible study groups in churches. Others gather in homes or restaurants. Every week, I attend four small groups: two 12-step groups, a men's group at Starbuck's, and another men's group that meets at another local restaurant.

Here's your assignment for today. Find a group, if you don't already have one. Start with your church. Look online. Then get in a group as soon as possible.

Day 47: 12-Step Group

God's Word for Today

You need to find recovery. But you can't do it alone. You need other people in your life; we all do.

Dr. Susan Whitbourne wrote an article that was published in *Psychology Today* on March 26, 2013, titled *15 Reasons You Need Friends*. At the end of the article, Whitbourne concludes, "You are a product of your friends, even if they are no longer your friends."

One of the things many addicts resist is joining a 12-step group. (I know, we've talked about this before, but some of us need to hear it several times before we jump in.) I hear it all the time. "I don't have anything in common with the group." "The group is secular, and not Christ-centered." "I may be seen walking into the building by someone who knows me."

> *"You are a product of your friends, even if they are no longer your friends."*

All of those statements may be true. But they are excuses – not reasons – to not join a group. After several years of successful recovery, I still attend two meetings a week. Why? I need the fellowship and accountability these groups offer.

Some of my most enjoyable moments have been spent in the stadium or arena, celebrating an Astros World Series win or a Rockets playoff win with thousands of people with whom I had virtually nothing in common other than our love for sports.

And some of my best recovery moments have come in the rooms where fellow addicts gather for support and encouragement.

There is actually a direct link from meaningful relationships to personal recovery. The Bible says, "Above all, love each other deeply, because love covers a multitude of sins" (1 Peter 4:8).

You have a problem for which there is hope. That hope is that you can find recovery. But you can't do it alone.

Today's Exercise

You should have been in a 12-step group since Day 14. Take a minute and write three blessings you have experienced in your SA, SAA, or CR meetings so far.

- _____
- _____
- _____

If you haven't yet found a 12-step group, you can identify a group today. Better yet, you can be in a group today – by phone, if not in person. Below, you will see some options. When you go to these websites, you will find locations and phone numbers for meetings.

Live Meetings

- Sexaholics Anonymous (SA): sa.org
- Sex Addicts Anonymous (SAA): saa-recovery.org
- Celebrate Recovery (CR): celebraterecovery.com

Phone Meetings

- SA: saphonemeeting.org
- SAA: saa-recovery.org (follow link to phone meetings)

Day 48: Church

God's Word for Today

Congratulations on your commitment to personal purity! There are two truths you must embrace early on: community and transparency.

Dietrich Bonhoeffer wrote, in *Life Together*, "The final obstacle to true Christian fellowship is the inability to be sinners together."

We must learn to be together, but togetherness is not enough. Sobriety is dependent on connecting with saints who know they are sinners. Then we must become comfortable with being sinners together.

It is impossible to overstate the need for transparent community in recovery. Alex Lerza, clinical psychologist and Certified Sex Addiction Therapist, says it like this: "The opposite of addiction is not sobriety, but relationship."

The secret sauce for the early church was their interconnectedness. "They devoted themselves to the apostles' teaching and the fellowship" (Acts 2:42). Most churches are big on teaching but weak on fellowship. We need both.

> **"The final obstacle to true Christian fellowship is the inability to be sinners together."**

Jesus died for the church. So there must be something to it. Notice that the church did not just meet occasionally; they were "devoted" to the gathering. And attending church is not a suggestion, but a commandment (Hebrews 10:25).

In recovery, you need community. And there is no better example of community than the local church.

Today's Exercise

The Bible speaks of three God-given institutions: the family, government, and church. Sadly, there is a diminishing commitment to the church – even among professing followers of Jesus Christ. It is not my job to convince you of the importance of the church. God has already made his case in Scripture and continues to do so through the Holy Spirit.

Our job here is to encourage you to do what you already know. Find a local church and commit your talents, time, and treasures to that church.

So what should you look for in a church? Here are a few suggestions.

1. Biblical preaching
2. Christ-centered
3. Meaningful worship
4. Sound biblical doctrine
5. Safe and effective childcare
6. Multiple small group options
7. Opportunities for service
8. Strong prayer ministry

The local church will be one of your greatest resources and sources of encouragement for your recovery. Write the name of the church you will attend this weekend.

Church: _____

Day 49: The Final Piece

God's Word for Today

Born in Budapest in 1897, George Szell was one of the most gifted pianists in the world. But no one remembers George Szell the pianist. They remember George Szell the conductor.

By age 20, Szell was conducting the Strasbourg Opera. By 27, he led the Berlin State Opera, and by 35, he had migrated to the United States and become lead conductor at the Metropolitan Opera House in New York City. For 25 years, Szell was recognized as the world's greatest conductor.

What was the key to Szell's success? One thing, he said. Early in life, "I decided to not focus on being the best pianist, but to help others be the best."

> "The best way to secure your own sobriety is to help others secure theirs."

In recovery, we can only go so far if we don't pour our lives into others. The most sober people I know are the ones who do the most to sponsor newcomers, make calls, and give back. As we say in every 12-step meeting, "The measure we gave was the measure we got back."

Your community is not complete until you include someone else who needs you. Give them your time and your wisdom. You will discover that the best way to secure your own sobriety is to help others to secure theirs.

This is a biblical principle. The Bible says, "There will never cease to be poor in the land. Therefore, I command you to open wide your hand to your brother, to the needy and to the poor in your land" (Deuteronomy 15:11).

Today's Exercise

W.H. Auden said, "We are all here to help others. Why they are here, I have no idea." In his humorous way, Auden makes a good point. That is why we are here – to help others.

It is never too soon to give back. You can help set up the room for an SA meeting. You can reach out to newcomers. You can stay after meetings to encourage someone else. Within a few months of entering recovery, you can begin to sponsor others. Below, list five ways you can give back by helping someone else.

1. _____

2. _____

3. _____

4. _____

5. _____

WEEK 8

TRIGGERS

"I can resist everything except temptation."
- Oscar Wilde

Day 50: H.A.L.T.

God's Word for Today

To maintain your sobriety, you must learn to deal with triggers. Triggers are those situations that arise - sometimes without notice and due to no fault of your own - with the potential of derailing in a moment what you have spent years to build.

Paul often found himself up against such temptations. That's why he would say, "I do not understand what I do. For what I want to do I do not do, but what I hate I do" (Romans 7:15).

Triggers take many forms, but an old formula in recovery material will be useful to you. It's called "H.A.L.T." We tend to run into trouble when we are

H = Hungry
A = Angry
L = Lonely
T = Tired

"God has more ropes and ladders and tunnels out of pits than you can conceive. Wait. Pray without ceasing. Hope."

The good news is that, while temptation can jump up at any moment, you can protect yourself against the "big four." Take care of yourself. Eat healthy so you won't be hungry. Confess your bitterness so you won't be angry. Build relationships so you won't be lonely. Get rest so you won't be tired.

John Piper said it well. "Darkness comes. In the middle of it, the future looks blank. You will argue with yourself that there is no way forward. But with God, nothing is impossible. He has more ropes and ladders and tunnels out of pits than you can conceive. Wait. Pray without ceasing. Hope."

You'll fight triggers for the rest of your life. But in Christ there is hope. But never forget your triggers. Never forget H.A.L.T.

Today's Exercise

The number of temptations and triggers is countless. But you can certainly remember H.A.L.T. This is a memorable formula to keep in mind consistently. But let's narrow it down some more. While we all struggle when we are hungry, angry, lonely, or tired, each of us runs into more trouble with some of these triggers than others.

You need to constantly be aware of your primary triggers. So put these in order, from the most difficult to the least. Number them from 1 to 4.

H = Hungry _____

A = Angry _____

L = Lonely _____

T = Tired _____

Day 51: The Loneliest Number

God's Word for Today

Dr. Shahram Heshmat wrote an excellent article, *Addiction as a Disease of Isolation*. He makes the case for isolation as a leading contributor to addiction.

He writes, "Since insecurity-attached individuals doubt the availability and support of others, they use other tactics to mitigate and control negative effects. One compensatory strategy is attachment to non-human targets (for example, objects and materialism). In other words, they substitute relationships with objects for relationships with people."

> *"You are only alone if you choose to be. Be aware – your isolation feeds your addiction. And that never ends well."*

Heshmat is suggesting that in our addiction, we avoid personal connections. We isolate. And that never ends well. Consider the prophet Elijah, for example.

"The Israelites have rejected your covenant, torn down your altars, and put your prophets to death with the sword. I am the only one left, and now they are trying to kill me, too" (1 Kings 19:10).

Elijah actually had 7,000 others ready to stand by his side. But in the face of difficulty, he retreated into isolation and depression. The fact is, isolation is a choice. You are only alone if you choose to be. Be aware – your isolation feeds your addiction. And that never ends well.

What Solomon said thousands of years ago still applies today. "Whoever isolates himself seeks his own desire; he rejects sound judgment" (Proverbs 18:1).

Today's Exercise

Isolation is at the root of all addictions. But as we mature, we recognize that isolation is not just a condition. It is a choice. And isolation is a demon that needs to be defeated.

Hear the words of John Lennon's hit song from 1970. "People say we've got it made. Don't they know we're so afraid? We're afraid to be alone. Everybody got to have a home."

Here's your assignment for today. It comes in two parts.

Part A – Write your story.

If you think about it, you will find an instance (or more than one) of isolation in your childhood. Write it down. What is one situation which drove you into isolation as a child? Be specific.

_____
_____
_____
_____
_____

Part B – Name a date and person.

In order to break the cycle of isolation, you need to connect with other people. So think of a person (same sex) with whom you can share a lunch, dinner, or casual activity. Get beyond yourself. Name one person you might contact, and an activity to share.

Name: _____

Activity: _____

Day 52: Fantasy Island

God's Word for Today

In the 1980s, there was a mind-numbing show on ABC called *Fantasy Island*. It was about people who went off to an island that represented a utopian existence. Each person was granted their greatest fantasy. Then reality hit and they had to return to their old lives.

Addicts try to live their entire lives on Fantasy Island. It is an escape, a coping mechanism. More than that, it is a trigger that leads to acting out.

Here's why . . .

What we think today is what we do tomorrow. And what we do tomorrow is who we become after that. It all starts in the head. And one of the biggest mistakes people make early in their recovery is to minimize their thought lives.

Studies show that a leading instrument of relapse is sexual fantasy. One specific study found that addicts spend 42 times more time on their phone apps and social media than in counseling. This, of course, opens the mind to all kinds of intrusive thoughts.

"One of the biggest mistakes people make early in their recovery is to minimize their thought lives."

So what's so bad about fantasy? We find one answer from Israeli psychologist Dr. Gurit E. Birnbaum. In an article published in the *Personality and Social Psychology Bulletin*, Birnbaum shares her work. She conducted a case study of 48 married couples. She discovered the reason we fantasize: "Sexual fantasy is a way to avoid intimacy."

Paul spoke to this danger with clarity. "Clothe yourself with the presence of the Lord Jesus Christ. And don't let yourself think about ways to indulge evil desires" (Romans 13:14).

In other words, get off Fantasy Island.

Today's Exercise

Dr. Brian Mustanski, author of *The Sexual Continuum*, did an extensive study of 283 students between the ages of 18 and 25. They were asked to record the number of thoughts they had about sex, food, and sleep over a one-week period. The conclusions were that, on average, young men think about sex 18.6 times per day, while women do the same 9.9 times per day.

Most would probably assume that these are the prime years for fantasy. But clearly, sexual thoughts and fantasy intrude all of our minds. But the bigger question is not how often you think about sex, but what you do with those thoughts.

I would argue that fantasies cannot be eliminated, but they can be mitigated. Let me suggest five exercises for you to try the next time you find yourself on the cusp of fantasy.

1. **Make a call**: Reach out to your sponsor or someone in your recovery group as soon as possible. This will help to move your mind to a healthier place.
2. **Pop and Pray**: When the thought begins to take root, stop everything and say a prayer – for yourself and the person about whom you may be fantasizing.
3. **Remember the 20-minute rule**: In 20 minutes, the temptation will likely pass. So stay busy for the next 20 minutes.
4. **Tell yourself the end of the story**: When you fantasize, you probably imagine a scenario that leads to sexual fulfillment through means that breach your moral code. Remind yourself of how this would end – guilt and shame included.
5. **3rd Step Prayer**: Pray, "God, I offer myself to you, to build with me and do with me as you will. Relieve me of the bondage of self, that I may better do your will. Take away my difficulties, that victory over them will bear witness to those I would help of your power, your love, and your way of life."

Day 53: The Great Curse

God's Word for Today

The Tartar tribes of central Asia spoke a certain curse against the enemy. They didn't call for their enemy's swords to rust or for their people to die of disease. Instead, they said, "May you stay in one place forever."

The best way to assure that you will never get better is by staying in one place forever. Standing still will get you nowhere.

Recovery is all about movement, making changes, and climbing the next hill. I know guys who have been in successful recovery for decades. "What did you do when you finished the twelve steps?" I asked one of them. "I started over" was his reply.

The Book of 2 Chronicles records the completion of King Solomon's temple and the split kingdom, with a focus on the Southern Kingdom of Judah. The writer chronicles (hence the name of the book) the activities of 19 kings, some good and some bad. One of those kings was Asa, who sought to be faithful to God when others around him were not.

"Recovery is all about movement, making changes, and climbing the next hill."

God made this promise to the king: "But as for you, be strong and do not give up. Your work will be rewarded" (2 Chronicles 15:7).

In recovery there is a temptation to look back, give up, or stand still. But it is only in moving forward that we get well and stay well.

Today's Exercise

You are well past the half-way point in your 90 days of recovery. This is a good time for a check-up. Many grow stagnant in their recovery work, especially after a short period of success. As we saw in today's devotional, this is the greatest curse. You must keep working on your recovery – for life.

Today's exercise is a simple one. Recite two prayers that are key to lasting recovery, with a heart to keep moving forward every day.

The Serenity Prayer

*"God, grant me the serenity to accept the things I cannot change,
the courage to change the things that I can,
and the wisdom to know the difference."*

The 3rd Step Prayer

*"God, I offer myself to you, to build with me and do with me as
you will. Relieve me of the bondage of self, that I may better
do your will. Take away my difficulties, that victory
over them may bear witness to those I would help
of your power, your love, and your way of life."*

Day 54: Bankrupted by Success

God's Word for Today

Bud Post won $16.2 million in the Pennsylvania state lottery. He figured he was set for life. But his ex-girlfriend successfully sued him for a share of his winnings. And Bud's brother hired a hit man to kill him, hoping to inherit some of the fortune. Sadly, Bud's troubles didn't end there. Due to his fulfilling repeated requests for debt relief from family and friends, plus making a large investment in a failed business venture, Bud found himself over $1 million in debt within a year of winning the lottery. By the time he reached retirement age, the former multimillionaire was surviving on $450 a month and food stamps.

> *"The more you have, the less you trust."*

Bud Post is not alone. Within five years of winning the jackpot, one-third of all lottery winners declare bankruptcy. Too often, we put our trust in our own wisdom.

Wise old Solomon offered a better way. "Trust in the Lord with all your heart and lean not on your own understanding. In all your ways submit to him, and he will make your paths straight" (Proverbs 3:5-6).

I admit it. My spiritual gift is worry. I want to figure it out, measure it out, and then carry it out. I like to be in control. But this comes with a heavy price. Worry brings stress, while achieving nothing else.

Martin Luther said, "Pray, and let God worry."

That's good advice. Like Bud Post, you might win the lottery. But be warned: the more you have, the less you trust. And recovery is a spiritual process, one that requires complete abandonment to your Higher Power. Remember, it was trusting in your own resources and ideas that got you into trouble in the first place.

Today's Exercise

Sometimes, success can be the enemy of recovery. That's why most people don't get into recovery until they hit bottom. Their addiction has to first cost them something. And many times, those who begin attending meetings and working the steps don't last – because their spouse no longer holds them accountable, or they haven't really hit bottom yet.

So what is the answer? Obviously, it is not recommended to hit bottom just to become desperate. But it is recommended that you never lose sight of the price you may pay if you stray from your program.

Here's today's exercise. Determine to build a relationship with someone you have met in your recovery program, who has lost much. Do this for two reasons. First, it is good to help others. Be there for that person.

But there is another benefit. By getting to know someone who has lost much, this will be a living example for you to consider as you work your own recovery.

One person who I know has paid a steep price for his addiction is _____. I will seek to make contact with him/her this week.

Day 55: The Devil's Workshop

God's Word for Today

"David sent someone to find out about her [Bathsheba]" (2 Samuel 11:3).

Before David got into trouble with Bathsheba he got into trouble with himself. At a time when other kings were off at war, David chose to stay back in his very luxurious man cave.

It was just another spring night at the palace, and boredom set in. The couch made no demands and the remote fit snugly in his hand. David hit the channel button at random until an alluring flicker caught his eye. Reverse. Stop. Pause. He zoomed in to watch a tantalizing scene – an intimate candlelit spa. And the king could almost smell the candle wax and bath oil. Although the cool evening air caused a slight haze to rise from the water, the bather's physical attributes were unmistakable.

"David got into trouble because he didn't get into anything else."

Long before channel surfing, King David knew about channel surfing. Bored, he became curious. Curious, he became enticed. Enticed, he became trapped. Then, within minutes, it seemed like hours. And it was too late. The sin had been committed.

David got into trouble because he didn't get into anything else.

Anne Baxter said, "Idleness is a constant sin, and labor is a duty. Idleness is the devil's home for temptation and for unprofitable, distracting musings; while labor profits others and ourselves."

King David is us. Idleness. Boredom. Being in the wrong place. Or simply not being in the right place. They get us all into trouble. And then trouble gets into us.

Today's Exercise

You need a project. You need to stay busy. In recovery, it is critical that we never take anything for granted. Addicts get into the most trouble when they put life in neutral. A vacation or down time put their sobriety at risk.

So if you see idleness creeping into your life, do something about it! But let's be clear. Don't take on a new project just to stay *extra* busy. *Regular* busy is enough.

Below, check any examples of projects that you think might be helpful to your sobriety.

- Sponsoring a 12-step newcomer _____
- Church mission trip _____
- Neighborhood project _____
- New hobby _____
- Classes at a local community college _____
- Date night with your spouse _____
- Learning a new trade _____
- Reading a new book _____
- Recovery Day _____
- Getting a pet _____
- Reconnecting with an old friend _____
- Joining a gym _____

Day 56: Complacency

God's Word for Today

During a battle in the Civil War, one of General Longstreet's officers approached him to say that he couldn't obey Longstreet's order to bring up his men to the line of battle, as the enemy was too strong. Longstreet responded with sarcasm.

He said, "Very well. Never mind. Just let them stay where they are. The enemy will advance, and that will spare you the trouble."

If we are to maintain our sobriety, we must engage the enemies of our recovery every day: temptation, fantasy, past failures, and – most of all – complacency.

> *"Engage the enemy – or the enemy will engage you."*

An Alpine guide died on a mountainside in Europe. At that spot a sign reads, "He died climbing." May that be said of each of us.

A.W. Tozer said, "Complacency is a deadly foe of all spiritual growth. Acute desire must be present or there will be no manifestation of Christ to his people. He waits to be wanted."

Solomon was right: "Through laziness, the rafters sag; because of idle hands, the house leaks" (Ecclesiastes 10:18).

Engage the enemy or the enemy will engage you. Complacency is not an option. If your house is leaking, it's time to plug the hole.

It may sound crazy to describe complacency as a trigger, but it is one of the most powerful triggers in addiction. Learn from the words of General Longstreet. There is a civil war raging within all of us. There is a constant fight between doing what we know is right and giving into temptation. You can engage the enemy – or wait for the enemy to engage you.

Today's Exercise

It is estimated that 60 percent of sex addicts have at least one other addiction as well. In your final exercise on triggers, think about your other struggles. Porn and sex addiction are not unrelated to the rest of your life. It all works together. Sometimes, complacency sets in when we get on top of one addiction, but neglect others.

Some of us suffer from substance addictions, while others' issues are tied to compulsive behaviors. You need to become aware of your addictions, beyond sex and porn. Check the ones you struggle with from this incomplete list, then surrender them to God.

- Alcohol _____
- Tobacco _____
- Opioids _____
- Prescription drugs _____
- Illegal drugs _____
- Food _____
- Gambling _____
- Social media _____
- Shopping _____
- Video games _____
- Fitness _____
- Other _____
- Other _____
- Other _____
- Other _____

WEEK 9

GUARDRAILS

"Hollywood is portrayed in this super glamorous way, but when I see pictures of actresses going off the rails, it doesn't surprise me at all."
- Minnie Driver

Day 57: The 3-Second Rule

God's Word for Today

The focus for this week is boundaries. To stay sober, you will need to put guardrails in place to avoid driving off the cliff. A guardrail is always in the safe zone. When you drive up a mountain, you not only avoid going off the edge; you stay as far inside the guardrails as possible.

The first guardrail for sobriety is the eyes. There was a man in the Bible named Job. Job had experienced incredible highs and devastating lows. Through it all, he embraced his commitment to remain pure. So Job put a plan in place to confront temptation. This was Job's guardrail: "I made a covenant with my eyes that I would not look lustfully at a young woman" (Job 31:1).

> **"Lust writes checks it cannot cash."**

Digital marketing experts estimate that most Americans are exposed to thousands of advertisements every day. In total, we take in 15,000 visual images per day. From early on, we are inundated with visual – and often sexual – images. We don't have to go looking for them. They find us.

On average, a boy's first viewing of pornography comes by the age of 11. And it only escalates from there.

Recovery is not just about not acting out. It is about progressive victory over lust. Lust writes checks it cannot cash. It leaves us bankrupt and alone. Presbyterian theologian Frederick Buechner said it like this: "Lust is the craving for salt of a man who is dying of thirst."

Lust starts with the eyes. Visual images lodge in our minds like nothing else. The best way to win the battle is to not take in the images in the first place. And that means making a covenant with our eyes.

Today's Exercise

Stephen Arterburn encourages us to "bounce the eyes." The idea is that when we see an enticing image, we immediately move our eyes away in another direction. It is inarguable that bouncing the eyes starves addiction and feeds recovery.

But I offer a variation on this. I call it the "3-second rule." Here's how it works.

Whenever you see something that is tempting or sensual, count to three. Make sure you have moved your eyes away by the time you get to "three."

There are two reasons the "3-second rule" works. First, by counting, your mind is refocused. It is much harder to maintain eye contact with an alluring subject while counting "1-2-3." The "3-second rule" is a healthy distraction.

Second, the "3-second rule" is more realistic and definable than "bouncing the eyes." For some, "bouncing" means to look elsewhere instantaneously. Others allow themselves several seconds to take in the image first. You are more likely to find success by drawing a clear line. I suggest drawing that line at three seconds. You can (and should) look away in less than three seconds. But never take longer than three seconds.

Try the "3-second rule" today. It works.

Day 58: Watchman

God's Word for Today

Putting up the necessary guardrails involves accountability. Stephen Covey writes, "Accountability breeds response-ability." In other words, you are responsible for your own sobriety, but you can't do it alone. The only thing harder than maintaining personal purity with the support of others is to do it on your own.

The ancient prophet Ezekiel was given a critical assignment. God appointed him as "watchman" over his people in the face of enemy attack. God told him, "I have made you a watchman for the people of Israel; so hear the word I speak and give them warning from me" (Ezekiel 33:7).

Matthew Henry describes this role of the watchman. He is "to discover the approaches and advances of the enemy, and to give notice to them immediately by the sound of a trumpet."

To enjoy lasting sobriety, you need to have a watchman and you need to be a watchman.

"The only thing harder than maintaining personal purity with the support of others is to do it on your own."

First, you need to have a watchman. This is a sponsor or someone else with successful long-term recovery. They will see the threat to your sobriety that you might miss.

Second, you need to be a watchman. Even in your earliest days of recovery, you can help others. Look for a meeting newcomer who needs a friend. Share what is working for you. Help him to recognize the hidden pitfalls to early sobriety.

A watchman – it's who you need and it's who you are, if you hope to achieve and maintain lasting sobriety.

Today's Exercise

Watchmen come in many shapes and sizes. They can be sponsors, prayer partners, best friends, pastors, or old chums from high school. But I have a better idea.

Covenant Eyes.

When you subscribe to Covenant Eyes, your computer and other electronic devices will be monitored. You will select a willing partner who will receive a weekly report on your Internet search activity.

There is a small fee to use Covenant Eyes or other similar monitoring companies. But the price is well worth it.

Why does Covenant Eyes work? There are two reasons.

First, the accountability is an obvious guardrail. This person should not be your husband or wife. He or she needs to be someone you can trust, and who will take it seriously.

Second, as valuable as the actual accountability is, just as valuable is the fact that you know you are being "watched." This makes many addicts think twice before viewing unsavory material on their phone or computer.

If you viewed porn sites or dating platforms online in the past, or if you think there is any *chance* you might be tempted to do so in the future, Covenant Eyes is for you.

Day 59: Manifesto

God's Word for Today

It is known as the "Modesto Manifesto." Here's the story. In 1948, Billy Graham held a series of evangelistic meetings in Modesto, California. His team of Cliff Barrows, Grady Wilson, and George Beverly Shea agreed to "avoid any situation that would have even the appearance of compromise or suspicion." Among other things, this meant that none of them would ever be alone with a woman (over lunch, in an office, or even in an elevator) other than their wives.

This is the framework for perhaps the most important guardrail you can put in place.

> **"We should not even put ourselves in the position to do something wrong."**

The Bible says to "flee youthful lusts" (2 Timothy 2:22). That doesn't mean to back away from lust or take a quick glance and look in the other direction. It means run! And don't look back.

I love antique cars. When you go to a show, you will see beautiful cars surrounded by ropes. There will generally be a sign that says something like "Look, but don't touch!" I do what everybody does. I get as close to the rope as possible, and I peer into the car. I often take pictures so I can go back and look at the car again.

That's okay with cars, but not with the opposite sex. It is natural to get as close to the rope (guardrail) as we can. But looking can be as intoxicating as touching.

The lesson from the "Modesto Manifesto" is not that we should not do anything wrong. The lesson is that we should not even put ourselves in *position* to do something wrong.

Today's Exercise

You need your own version of the "Modesto Manifesto." I suggest you draw up some guidelines by which you will live your life. Set the boundaries you will not violate. Put up the ropes you will not cross.

I suggest three examples.

First, never be alone with a woman other than your wife (or if you are a woman – a man other than your husband). Don't waver on this. Stick to it at all times.

Second, if you have a private office, install a small window into the door, so others can look in.

Third, connect your wife with other women in your life. Keep her picture on your desk. Give her access to your contacts with women at work. Invite her to come by the office from time to time. Make your marriage and family common knowledge among your friends and among those with whom you work.

You need your own "manifesto." Write one below.

My "Manifesto": _____
_____
_____
_____
_____
_____
_____
_____

Day 60: Say No

God's Word for Today

On the wall of the Betty Ford Clinic you will find these words: "Self-care is about setting boundaries." A lack of boundaries is at the root of every addiction. Not having secure boundaries is what got you into your mess. In recovery, it is critical to set boundaries you will not cross.

Every person's recovery calls for its own set of boundaries. The alcoholic may need to avoid parties that serve mixed drinks. The gambler may need to avoid casinos. The sex addict may need to cut off cable television or access to the Internet. The shopaholic may need to not shop alone.

"Addicts get into trouble by saying 'yes' too much."

Just as Lot cast his tent "toward Sodom" (Genesis 13:12), we are naturally drawn by the tease. We want to get as close to the edge as we can without going over it.

We need to learn to say "no" and walk away.

Warren Buffet said, "The difference between successful people and really successful people is that really successful people say 'no' to just about everything."

Addicts get into trouble by saying "yes" too much. It's okay to say "no." In fact, Megan LeBoutillier wrote a whole book about it, by the title of *No Is a Complete Sentence*.

In recovery, you need to learn to say "no" to certain people, places, and predicaments. You need a new route home from work, a new set of friends, and new guardrails in how you spend your money.

LeBoutillier is right. "No" is a complete sentence.

Today's Exercise

In setting boundaries, you need to learn the art of saying "no." But recovery will only come as you equip yourself with the right tools to say 'no.' Let me suggest two of these, as found in Stephen Arterburn's work.

First, you need the sword. Arterburn identifies Job's words as the sword: "I have made a covenant with my eyes" (Job 31:1). When we see an attractive jogger or waitress or a seductive billboard, we need to go on the offensive, and say, "No, I have made a covenant with my eyes. I will not look at you."

Second, you need a shield. Quote the words of Paul: "Flee from sexual immorality. You are not your own" (1 Corinthians 6:18). You do not have the authority to take in that extra look or to cross that boundary.

In order to learn your sword and shield, write each of these verses below:

Job 31:1 _____
_____
_____

1 Corinthians 6:18 _____
_____
_____

Day 61: Intrusive Thoughts

God's Word for Today

In the sheep country of New Mexico, shepherds were losing lots of lambs in the wintertime. The problem was, the ewes were taking their lambs out to graze late in the day, and when it started to snow, the temperatures would drop below freezing. But the ewes were unaware of the danger to the young lambs and would continue to graze, and many of the lambs froze to death.

The shepherds came to realize the problem. The ewes were unaware of the danger because they were covered in such thick wool that they didn't feel the drop in temperature. The shepherds came up with a unique solution. They sheared the top of the ewes' heads. That way, when the temperature would drop, the ewes felt it and headed back to the barn, with their lambs following behind.

"It isn't enough to avoid bad thoughts; we must embrace positive ones."

Addiction works that way. Most of us were in trouble before we even knew it. How does this happen? Where does the trouble begin?

It begins in the mind.

The key, Paul said, is to "take every thought captive" (2 Corinthians 10:5). Too often, we try to not focus on seductive thoughts, but we stop there. It isn't enough to avoid bad thoughts; we must embrace positive ones. It is only when we fill our minds with positive thoughts that we can fend off the temptations that so easily carry us off into the depths of our addiction.

The slide into addiction is subtle. At first, we don't even notice it. But the inevitable end is destructive. It all begins with a battle in the mind . . . a battle that must be won.

Today's Exercise

What you think today, you become tomorrow. Solomon warned, "Above all else, guard your heart" (Proverbs 4:23). Paul said, "Set your minds on things above, not on earthly things" (Colossians 3:2). Our real battle is not physical, but mental.

We all battle intrusive thoughts from time to time. What is critical is that you have a battle plan in place before you need it. Let me suggest six tips.

1. **Pray**. Every day, repeat the Serenity Prayer, the 3rd Step Prayer, and the 7th Step Prayer.
2. **Remember the end game**. When you are tempted to act out, think through the entire process, focusing on the end – the feeling of shame and guilt if you relapse.
3. **Make a call**. Call your sponsor or someone else in recovery. Stay on the phone until your mind is refocused. Never go through the battle alone.
4. **Practice the 20-minute principle**. In about 20 minutes, the urge will have passed, whether you acted on it or not. So divert your mind for just 20 minutes.
5. **Maintain an anti-boredom list**. Our minds wander when we are bored. So be prepared to divert your mind to something else: financial planning, your next vacation, or something else that demands rigorous thought.
6. **Exercise**. Engage your body and mind in something other than your intrusive thoughts. What you do physically will affect you mentally.

Day 62: Get Fit

God's Word for Today

One of the guardrails many neglect is physical fitness. When we are unhealthy physically, this affects all of life. Paul recognized the benefits of physical exercise (1 Timothy 4:8). He reminds us that our bodies are God's temple (1 Corinthians 6:19). While we tend to compartmentalize life into the physical, spiritual, emotional, and mental, God makes no such distinction. He cares about the total person. It is all connected.

> *"Nutritional therapy can significantly help those recovering from addictions."*

Elijah was a test case in how the physical affects all else. His powerful ministry went into a tailspin, marked by mental anguish and depression. In his depression he lost his appetite.

Then the angel of the Lord stepped in. Notice God's first words to Elijah. He didn't tell him to pray more or to get his heart right. The angel said, "Get up and eat" (1 Kings 19:5).

Elijah got depressed when he didn't eat right. He lost his focus and drive. This is a real problem in America, where two-thirds of us are medically overweight or obese. A poor diet contributes to high cholesterol, high blood triglycerides, type-2 diabetes, high blood pressure, strokes, heart disease, gallbladder disease, cancer, osteoarthritis, skin problems, and – depression. And we know where depression leads.

David Wiss, founder of Nutrition in Recovery, concludes, "Mounting evidence points to one emerging consensus: nutritional therapy can significantly help those recovering from addictions."

To live right, you must eat right. And you must exercise right and sleep right. Otherwise, you can't be well.

Today's Exercise

The physical affects everything else, including your addiction. It is critical that you focus on the things that bring immediate sobriety: going to meetings, getting a sponsor, spiritual disciplines, etc. But don't neglect the physical. Here is a checklist of some of the things that demand your attention. Write one thing you can do to improve in each area that is currently a weakness.

1. Exercise: _____

2. Diet: _____

3. Sleep: _____

4. Doctor's visit: _____

5. Dental appointment: _____

6. Stress reduction: _____

7. Rest: _____

8. Other: _____

Day 63: Travel Plan

God's Word for Today

I remember it as if it happened yesterday. The date was November 5, 1994. The heavyweight champion of the world was a fighter named Michael Moorer. He had never lost a fight. Standing across the ring was a former champion who had not won a significant fight in nearly 20 years. His name was George Foreman.

At age 45, Foreman did not appear to be a significant threat to the champion. And as expected, Moorer dominated the fight, building an overwhelming lead on all three of the judges' scorecards entering the final round.

> *"You might be ahead on points right now, but don't let up until the fight is over."*

And then it happened. Foreman landed a single, devastating blow. Moorer never saw it. The champ went down, and he never got up.

That's how addiction hits us. We can cruise through life, and then, when we don't expect it, we lose our sobriety in a moment. Often, as with Moorer, the attack is not seen.

One of the most vulnerable times for each of us is when we travel. It is when we are out of our normal routines that we are susceptible to an attack from an unexpected source.

We must never lose our focus. The Bible says, "Let he who thinks he stands be careful, lest he fall" (1 Corinthians 10:12). In other words, never take a single day of sobriety for granted – especially when you are outside of your normal routine. The enemy is coming for you. You might be ahead on points right now, but don't let up until the fight is over.

Today's Exercise

When you travel, your sobriety is at an increased risk for two reasons. First, you will have less accountability. Second, you will be out of your normal routine, which includes established recovery activities that will be hard to maintain.

So let's get real practical. Below is a "Travel Guide." For the next time you travel, you need to prepare to do as much of this as possible, *before you leave home.*

1. **Tell someone**. Let your sponsor or accountability partner know you will be traveling. Then check in with him or her on a daily basis.
2. **Find a meeting**. If at all possible, attend at least one SA or SAA meeting per week while you are on the road. Go to their websites before you leave home, to find the meeting you will attend. If none fits your schedule, plan a time to participate in a phone meeting.
3. **Avoid adult TV options**. Call ahead. Make sure that your hotel room will not have free adult channels available.
4. **Call your spouse**. Commit to calling her frequently, and to being available to receive her calls.
5. **Bring recovery books**. Take your SA or SAA book or other reading material on your trip. Read just two or three pages each morning.
6. **Recite the three prayers**. Each day, recite the Sobriety Prayer, the 3rd Step Prayer, and the 7th Step Prayer.
7. **Make a call**. Make one call per day, to your sponsor or someone else in your recovery program.
8. **Don't isolate**. If you feel lonely in your hotel room, go to the fitness room. Avoid the bar or any other places where you might meet potential acting out partners.

WEEK 10

HOUSEKEEPING

"The day I worry about cleaning my house is the day Sears comes out with a riding vacuum cleaner."
- Roseanne Barr

Day 64: Dump the Stash

God's Word for Today

John Piper tells the story about the time he had a fight with his wife early in their marriage. He needed a break from the argument, so he left the house to take the garbage down the street to the pick-up spot. He says, "As I walked down the driveway toward the street where we set the garbage, the sun broke through the morning clouds. To this day, the profoundness of that moment grips me. Here I was huffing and puffing with my hurt feelings and desires for vindication, and God, who had every right to strike me dead, opened the window of heaven and covered me with pleasure. I recall stopping and letting it soak in. It felt like paradise – garbage in hand."

> *"We all have garbage we need to take out."*

The Bible says, "The heavens declare the glory of God; the skies proclaim the work of his hands . . . In the heavens God has pitched a tent for the sun" (Psalm 19:1, 4).

This week's theme is "housekeeping." Congratulations on entering week ten in recovery. Now is a good time to shore some things up, to make sure your house is in order.

What was true for John Piper is also true for you and me. We all have garbage we need to take out. We need to take it to the cross, God's pick-up spot. That's where we lay our garbage down.

There is an interesting promise for those of us willing to release our garbage. We experience God's glory and his redeeming grace in the process. God does not wait until we are garbage-free to reveal his glory. He has "pitched a tent" of blessing for each of us who are in the process of taking out the garbage.

What garbage are you hanging onto? Start bagging it up today, and take it to the cross.

Today's Exercise

No one puts their garbage in the living room for all to see. The same is true of addiction. Sexual addiction always involves secrets. While living in our addiction, we spend as much time trying to hide it or cover it up as we do acting out.

We must bring our garbage out into the open. Then we must take it to the curb/cross, and let it go. But first, we have to be willing to get rid of it – *all of it*. That's the only way our house will be in order.

Check the kinds of trash you need to take out. Then write the date you plan to do that – preferably today!

1. Printed pornography _____
2. Computer bookmarks _____
3. Downloaded porn images _____
4. Hidden phone numbers _____
5. Hidden cash _____
6. Sex paraphernalia/lingerie _____
7. Hidden contact information _____
8. Saved pictures/photographs _____
9. Old letters or emails _____

Date you will dump the stash: _____

Day 65: Turning the Page

God's Word for Today

Coach John Wooden used to tell his players, "Experience does you no good. It is learning from experience that makes the difference."

The Apostle Paul learned from his mistakes. After his friend John Mark had abandoned him during the first missionary journey, Paul wrote him off. He never gave him a second chance or traveled with him again. But late in his life, Paul recognized his folly. In his dying letter written from the cell of a prison, Paul wrote, "Bring Mark to me. He is helpful to me in my ministry" (2 Timothy 4:11).

> **"It's okay to visit the past, but it's not okay to live there."**

How could a man who had abandoned Paul be described as "helpful"?

The answer isn't that John Mark changed (though he did). The difference was that Paul had changed. He learned from his mistakes.

Rick Warren says, "We are products of our past, but we don't have to be prisoners of it." Johann Wolfgang von Goethe said it like this: "By seeking and blundering we learn."

The fact is, we all have a past. We all have made huge mistakes that we regret. And it's okay to visit the past, but it's not okay to live there.

Men and women in sex addiction recovery often struggle to move into their future out of shame over their past. As a part of your housekeeping work this week, you need to face your past, then learn to turn the page on it.

Today's Exercise

Let me suggest an exercise that will help you turn the page to a better future. Say goodbye to your addiction. Do it in the form of a letter. Take a few minutes to thank your addiction for teaching you the hard lessons of surrender and dependence on God. But also tell it that it no longer has control of your life.

Dear Addiction,

_____
_____
_____
_____
_____
_____
_____
_____
_____
_____
_____
_____

Signed,

_____

Day 66: Realignment

God's Word for Today

Charlie Brown commented on what it meant to have a good day. "I know it's going to be a good day when all the wheels on my shopping cart turn the same way."

If ever there was a time when our lives needed to be in alignment, it is in our personal recovery. That means having all our wheels headed in the same direction – therapy, meetings, prayer, working the steps, calling our sponsor, surrender, honesty. If we try to maintain sobriety with even one of the wheels out of alignment, we will live a life of constant frustration.

"Faith is taking the first step, even when you don't see the whole staircase."

The good news is the road to recovery is well-lit. "The Lord says, 'I will guide you along the best pathway for your life'" (Psalm 32:8). God is committed to your personal recovery.

Martin Luther King, Jr., said, "Faith is taking the first step, even when you don't see the whole staircase."

When I got into recovery, I didn't see the whole staircase. But I always saw the next step. And that is enough.

Part of housekeeping is getting your life in concert. You need to bring it all in alignment, as you love God with your heart, mind, body, and soul. You need to be proactive. Do the things that keep your cart headed in the right direction. Follow God's plan for your life – even when you can't see the whole staircase.

Today's Exercise

In recovery, it is typical to get things a bit out of alignment. We may still be doing many things well, but we tend to neglect some aspects of recovery. For example, we may be going to 12-step meetings, but not working the steps. Or we may be attending worship services, but not be praying much on our own.

Below, I will list a few of the things that you need to have in alignment for your recovery to maintain long-term traction. Number each item, from one to ten, in the order in which you feel you are being the most successful. Then take your bottom three and identify ways to bring them up to the same level as the other aspects of your recovery.

_____ Attending and benefitting from 12-step meetings

_____ Personal devotional time

_____ Personal fitness plan

_____ 12-step work

_____ Congregational worship

_____ Work with sponsor

_____ Connection with spouse

_____ Fantasy life

_____ Reading recovery material

_____ Custody of eyes

Day 67: Good Grief

God's Word for Today

Finding recovery does not equal losing pain. The problems are still there and the temptations are still real. We want the memories and wounds to heal instantaneously. But that rarely happens.

A prophet in the Old Testament came to God in absolute surrender. His name was Habakkuk. He prayed for God's blessings out of a pure heart. Habakkuk wasn't faking it. The change of his heart was real.

But God's blessings did not all come at once. There was still a period of pain that would serve as a test. And Habakkuk passed that test.

"Even though the fig trees have no blossoms, and there are no grapes on the vines; even though the olive crop fails, and the fields are empty and barren; even though the flocks die in the fields, and the cattle barns are empty, yet I will rejoice in the Lord! I will be joyful in the God of my salvation" (Habakkuk 3:17-18).

> *"Grief is in two parts. The first is loss. The second is the remaking of life."*

It's easy to live in sobriety when we are heavily rewarded. But it's what we do when our wife doesn't come home, when we still lose our job, when our friends still turn away that counts.

Recovery is its own reward. Yes, there will be a period of pain and grief, but that is just part of the healing process. A time of grief and loss is inevitable. But it can be good grief, if you let it.

Anne Rolphe said it best: "Grief is in two parts. The first is loss. The second is the remaking of life."

Today's Exercise

Grief is part of the housekeeping process. It is important to let your grief run a healthy course. Doug Weiss writes, in *101 Freedom Exercises*, "Sex addiction has probably been your best friend. It has told you that you were worthwhile. It accepted you no matter what. When you divorce yourself from your addiction, you will go through a grieving process."

It is important to identify your current grief stage, then to move on. Where are you right now? Circle that stage below.

1. **Shock**: This comes with the recognition that you have a serious problem. There is an overwhelming sense of nausea and disbelief. This stage usually passes quickly.
2. **Denial**: This stage can last for years. For some, it lasts forever. In this stage, the addict says, "Sure, I've made some mistakes, but I can control it."
3. **Anger**: This is the time when you start to admit to an addiction. There is a feeling of entitlement. Irrational thought becomes the norm, and mood swings abound.
4. **Bargaining**: Now the addict shifts the blame to his or her spouse. The addict rationalizes that he should be able to dabble in his addiction. Who's it going to hurt?
5. **Sorrow**: The truth begins to settle in. The addict laments the pain his addiction has brought to him and others. There is a powerful feeling of loss.
6. **Acceptance**: Finally, the addict owns his disease. He takes responsibility for his recovery and quits blaming others. Now he is ready to get healthy and move forward.

Day 68: Drawing Circles

God's Word for Today

The year was 1911. The South Pole was not the vacation paradise it is today. But a Norwegian explorer named Roald Amundsen changed all that when he set out to become the first man to reach the South Pole. While assembling his team, Amundsen chose expert skiers and dog handlers. His strategy was simple. The dogs would do most of the work as they pulled the group 15 to 20 miles a day. Rather than rely on their own strength, they would rely on the strength of the dogs. It worked, as Amundsen became the first man to reach the South Pole.

> *"The road to recovery is one of exploration."*

The road to recovery is one of exploration. None of us got it right the first time. And as long as we sought sobriety in our own strength, we found no recovery at all.

The key to lasting recovery is surrender to our Higher Power. As Roald Amundsen relied on the strength of his dogs, we must rely on the strength of our God.

King David wrote, "The Lord is the strength of my life; of whom shall I be afraid?" (Psalm 27:1).

Alexander MacLaren nailed it: "Only he who can say, 'The Lord is the strength of my life' can also say, 'Of whom shall I be afraid?'"

Dwight L. Moody used to tell people how to find God's blessings. He said, "Get alone on your knees. Then draw a circle around yourself. Get everyone in that circle right with God, and his blessings will follow."

Make that one of your housekeeping chores this week. Learn to rely on God's strength, and not your own. And learn the power of complete surrender.

Today's Exercise

It's time to do a floor exercise. Do the "Moody exercise." Find a place, sometime today, where you can be alone. Make it somewhere a bit out of the ordinary, if possible. It might be your closet, an outdoor spot, or some other place that holds great meaning for you.

Then get on your knees and draw an imaginary circle around yourself. Finally, get everyone in that circle right with God.

The point is to focus only on you and your need for surrender. Only when you can exit the circle with no unconfessed sin – only then can you walk in freedom and hope.

Before you do the circle exercise, think about it. What are some of the things you need to confess when you get on your knees inside that circle? List them below. Then go find your circle!

1. _____

2. _____

3. _____

4. _____

5. _____

Day 69: Letting Go

God's Word for Today

The Bible says a lot about forgiveness. We must forgive others to gain God's forgiveness (Matthew 6:14-15). If a sister repents, we are to forgive her (Luke 17:3). We are to forgive them an unlimited number of times (Luke 17:4). We are to be an instrument of forgiveness because we have already been an object of forgiveness (Ephesians 4:32). The God who forgives our sin also forgets our sin (Isaiah 43:25).

And then there's Colossians 3:13. "Bear with each other and forgive one another if any of you has a grievance against someone. Forgive as the Lord forgave you."

That's a tall order – forgive as the Lord forgives. What does that mean?

As a part of our housekeeping process, we must identify those people – starting with ourselves – who have hurt us. We offer our forgiveness.

The little country church where I preached my first revival had two brothers who were both deacons. They had a falling out. Each Sunday, one faction sat on the left side while the other faction sat on the right. Despite repeated attempts by the pastor and others, the brothers would not reconcile. They wanted no part of forgiveness. And today, that church no longer exists.

> **"We forgive because we have been forgiven."**

A refusal to forgive demonstrates a lack of self-awareness. We forgive because we have been forgiven. And in forgiving those who have injured us, we touch God. And he touches us. And the healing begins.

Today's Exercise

When you do housekeeping chores, you discover some things you might have forgotten. In recovery, that means going back to your childhood and making a list of those whom you need to forgive. Perhaps it is a relative at whose hands you suffered abuse. It might be an old friend or church. Make a list of those you need to forgive.

Keep two things in mind. First, start with yourself. Second, it is not enough to list these names. You must actually forgive them.

What does that mean? Forgiveness is a form of release. You are releasing them to God. This removes the power they have wielded over you. Let's get started. Write the names, then do the work of forgiveness.

- _____
- _____
- _____
- _____
- _____
- _____
- _____
- _____
- _____
- _____
- _____
- _____
- _____

Day 70: Mistakes

God's Word for Today

About 2500 years ago, Chinese philosopher Lao Tzu said, "If you do not change direction, you may end up where you are headed."

A modern philosopher said it like this: "If all you do is what you've done, then all you'll get is what you've got."

Both Lao Tzu and Yogi Berra got it right. Progress requires change. And that means learning from past mistakes.

The prince of prophets said, "See, I am doing a new thing! Now it springs up; do you not perceive it? I am making a new way" (Isaiah 43:19).

The easy way out is to change your circumstances. But that rarely works. Victor Frankl said, "When we are no longer able to change a situation, we must change ourselves."

> *"If you don't change direction, you may end up where you are headed."*

Every morning, you should pray the Serenity Prayer: "God, grant me the serenity to accept the things I cannot change, the courage to change the things I can, and the wisdom to know the difference." Don't miss the middle part. We must have the courage to change the things we can.

Gandhi said, "You must be the change you wish to see." You can't wait for change to come from the outside. It must come from within. So before you finish cleaning house, take a moment to identify the mistakes of your past that have yet to be addressed.

Today's Exercise

The road to recovery is paved with the mistakes of the past. Don't let them go to waste! Bring your mistakes to the light, then ask yourself, "How can I learn from this?" This will just be a partial list. Write down five mistakes of your past, but more importantly, the lesson you can learn from each mistake.

1. Mistake: _____
   Lesson learned: _____
   _____

2. Mistake: _____
   Lesson learned: _____
   _____

3. Mistake: _____
   Lesson learned: _____
   _____

4. Mistake: _____
   Lesson learned: _____
   _____

5. Mistake: _____
   Lesson learned: _____
   _____

WEEK 11

DISCLOSURE

"There are no secrets that time does not reveal."
- Jean Racine

"Everybody is like a moon, and has a dark side which he never shows to anybody."
- Mark Twain

Day 71: Your Story

God's Word for Today

One of the most important steps in recovery is also one of the most painful – disclosure. This step should not be done too early in the recovery process, which is why we have it in week eleven. But few elements will be more critical to your long-term success.

Disclosure is all about transparency, which is foundational to an authentic life. Research supports this belief. Dr. Helen Keane, writing for *Sage Journal*, says, "An authentic life is marked by transparency and consistency between our inner and outer selves."

"Total, complete, absolute transparency feeds recovery like nothing else."

Transparency begins with our relationship with God. We must admit the nature of our wrongs to him. But this is just the beginning. The 12 steps teach us that we must also admit our wrongs to another human being.

Paul said it like this: "Each of you must put off falsehood and speak truthfully to your neighbor, for we are all members of one family" (Ephesians 4:25).

Transparency is a building block to recovery. That is because addiction thrives in secrecy. Nothing kills the addiction like bringing it to the light. Total, complete, absolute transparency feeds recovery like nothing else.

In therapy, this process is called a clinical disclosure. We will talk about that more later this week. In 12-step work we call this "taking the First Step." And that will be today's exercise.

Today's Exercise

Your assignment today is to start a project, not finish it. It is called "taking the First Step." The assignment is to write out your personal story. You should consult with your sponsor if you have one, and make this a part of your 12-step work. Your story will be read to your group when you and your sponsor feel you are ready. This is the culmination of working Step 1.

Your story is that of your sexual history, going back to your childhood, and even your family history. Do not share specific names or places. Typically, this will be several pages in length and take at least 15-20 minutes to read to the group.

To make your story easy to organize and present, it should consist of three phases: your life before recovery, how you found recovery, and your life since. Below, jot down the high points for each. Then, start writing your story in detail as soon as possible, perhaps a page or so each night.

1. Your life before recovery
    a. _____
    b. _____
    c. _____

2. How you found recovery
    a. _____
    b. _____
    c. _____

3. Your life since you entered recovery
    a. _____
    b. _____
    c. _____

Day 72: Coming Clean

God's Word for Today

That great theologian Billy Joel said, "I'd rather laugh with the sinners than cry with the saints."

There is something to be said for laughing – even from the valley of addiction. Keeping things bottled up always makes matters worse. But to whom do we turn? Who do we tell? I know this. You better find that person, because keeping your struggle to yourself only leads to implosion from within.

> *"Confession opens up possibilities we would otherwise miss."*

Following his sin with Bathsheba, King David went through a period of cover-up. He hid his sin, and to make matters worse, he had Bathsheba's husband put to death in order to have her for himself. It was all a part of a master plan to cover up what he had done.

And that worked – until it didn't. David would soon acknowledge, "When I kept silent my bones roared" (Psalm 32:3). He was saying, "Until I confessed what I had done to God and one other person, the pain shot down to my bones."

Secrets make us sick.

Dr. Alex Lickerman wrote, in *Psychology Today*, "Confession opens up possibilities we would otherwise miss."

What possibilities are you missing because of your secrets? A closer walk with God? A real connection with another human being? It's time to get it all out. Tell someone. Then get ready to see possibilities you would otherwise never know.

Today's Exercise

In coming clean, it is important that we acknowledge the exact nature of our disease. It is not enough to just say, "I'm a sex addict." In meetings, you will hear others specify the ways in which they acted out. By bringing this to the light, they avoid secrets and shame.

To help you organize your thoughts, you will find five ways men and women act out sexually. Circle the ones that apply to you. Do not include healthy sex that occurs within marriage; this is about your addictive behaviors.

1. **Physical sex**: any mutually agreed upon sex with another person other than your spouse – including affairs and prostitutes

2. **Objectifying sex**: fixation on images or sex partners outside of marriage, while engaging in marital sex

3. **Masturbating sex**: done with oneself, with or without outside stimuli such as pornography

4. **Violating sex**: asking one's spouse to perform sex acts with which he or she is not comfortable

5. **Traumatizing sex**: carrying out the sex act against the will of the partner

Day 73: Potter's Hand

God's Word for Today

For the family who wants to keep a tidy home, housecleaning is never done. It is a process, not a project. I have the cleanest home ever, because Beth cleans – often. It is not enough to clean one's home; it must be cleaned regularly.

The same is true in addiction recovery. We must commit to constant cleaning. John Henry Newman said, "To live is to change, and to be perfect is to have changed often."

> *"Few addicts find recovery until they hit bottom."*

God said to the prophet, "Can I not be with you, Israel, as this potter does? Like clay in the hand of the potter, so are you in my hand, Israel" (Jeremiah 18:6).

Here's what happened. God told Jeremiah to visit the potter's shop to learn a valuable lesson. He found the potter working at the wheel. But the jar the potter made did not turn out as he had hoped. So the potter crushed it into a lump of clay and started over again.

Our problem is that when we are ready for God to remove our shortcomings, we still want to control the process. In recovery, that never works. Few addicts find recovery until they "hit bottom." They must be desperate enough to place themselves in the potter's hand.

Until you are willing for God to reshape you however he wants, recovery will be elusive. In recovery, we ask God to remove all of our shortcomings. It is spiritual housecleaning. And it is a critical building block to recovery.

Today's Exercise

Most of us give a partial disclosure at first. We only share what we think we have to share. We try to paint a picture that falls short of revealing our darkest moments and greatest defects. But partial disclosure is non-disclosure.

When the potter found a defect in his work, he crushed the clay and started from scratch. That is a picture of recovery. We must be crushed, even humiliated, before we are ready to let go completely.

What is the one event, relationship, or encounter that you are still hanging onto? You need to identify the moment no one knows about. Just as weeds need to be dug up by their roots, your past needs to be exposed – completely. You don't need to tell most people, but you do need to tell someone.

Take a minute to write it down. What is the thing you've done that you think – if anyone else knew – would kill any chance of you being truly loved and accepted? And before you write it down, remember this: *There is nothing you can ever do that will make God love you more, and there is nothing you can ever do that will make him love you less.*

Write your bottom line, worst moment, or greatest defect:
_____
_____
_____
_____
_____

Day 74: Add It Up

God's Word for Today

Edgar Allan Poe's short story, *The Tell-Tale Heart*, tells the gruesome story of a murderer who hides his victim's body under the floorboards of his house. He is so confident that he cannot be discovered that he invites police investigators into his house, where he cheerfully answers all of their questions, while standing just above the corpse.

Then the murderer hears the sound of a beating heart from below his feet. He wonders why the police don't seem to hear it as the beating gets louder. Though the officers know nothing, the man finally loses it and confesses his crime.

Geoffrey Chaucer said, "The guilty think all talk is of themselves." In other words, the guilty become consumed in the destitution of their souls.

"A man is crippled by his guilt and buried by his secrets."

The Bible says, "Whoever conceals his sins does not prosper, but the one who confesses and renounces them finds mercy" (Proverbs 28:13).

John Adams said, "Great is the guilt of an unnecessary war."

One of the most unnecessary wars is the one that rages in the heart of a man who has something to hide. A man is crippled by his guilt and buried by his secrets. The key to recovery is not living a sin-free life. It is outing our mistakes before they destroy us.

Learn to confess your sins. Share your struggles. Reveal your past. And in the process, embrace a God who loves, forgives, and is the creator of the second chance.

Today's Exercise

Every addiction costs the addict something. His losses can be counted in many ways: time lost, money spent, relationships shattered, jobs lost, reputation destroyed. It is sobering to measure the cost of one's addiction. But the benefits are many. For one, it is good for the addict to confront the insanity of his loss as evidence that his life is, after all, out of control. To the best of your ability, do the math. Count the cost of your addiction.

1. **Money**
    a. Porn purchases: $_____
    b. Sex services: $_____
    c. Legal fees: $_____
    d. Therapy: $_____
    e. Other: $_____
    f. Total: $_____

2. **Time**
    a. Time acting out: _____
    b. Hours lost at work: _____
    c. Time viewing porn: _____
    d. Time spent in fantasy: _____
    e. Time on dating sites: _____
    f. Other: _____
    g. Total: _____

3. **Relationships**
    a. Spouse: _____
    b. Children: _____
    c. Friends: _____
    d. Co-workers: _____

Day 75: To Tell the Truth

God's Word for Today

An international survey of 164 recovering sex addicts, conducted by Jennifer Schneider and Deborah Corley, concluded that a full disclosure is an integral part of lasting sobriety. No one ever resisted doing a clinical disclosure more than I did, but I have come to believe that it is one of the four most important elements of recovery (along with desperation, surrender, and community).

> *"Whoever conceals his sin does not prosper."*

Scripture says, "Whoever conceals his sin does not prosper, but the one who confesses and renounces them finds mercy" (Proverbs 28:13). Unfortunately, research concludes that only 30 percent of sex addicts who offer a disclosure to their spouse actually give a *full* disclosure.

So what is a disclosure? It is a written accounting of your sexual history, presented to your spouse under the supervision of a trained therapist. There are several components to a successful disclosure. First, it must include total honesty. Women treasure that above all else. Second, it must be done with a trained therapist. The therapeutic setting is a must.

Third, the disclosure must be complete. Do not do it in increments. Fourth, a good disclosure is accompanied by a commitment by both spouses to seek marital restoration for one year, regardless of what the disclosure reveals. And fifth, the disclosure should be followed by a polygraph, so the wounded spouse can be assured of knowing the full truth.

Today's Exercise

I have come to believe the polygraph is an essential part to true disclosure. Every addict with whom I have worked who strongly resisted taking a polygraph did it for the same reason – they weren't ready to come completely clean. And as Dr. Milton Magness says in *Stop Sex Addiction*, "A disclosure that is less than 100 percent honest and complete is not a disclosure, but just another deception."

The purpose of a polygraph is to give the addict a chance to prove his honesty. It provides a reset. What most men fail to understand is that in the absence of knowing it all, their wives will imagine things that are almost always far worse than the actual reality.

Generally, the polygraph will allow for four or five relevant questions that are supplied by the therapist with the aid of the spouse. And the test is administered during the disclosure process, in the counseling setting.

So, for the addict, it comes down to one question. If your spouse requests it, are you willing to provide a clinical disclosure that includes a polygraph?

Yes _____

No _____

Day 76: Amends

God's Word for Today

One of the keys to addiction recovery is making amends when possible, and when doing so does not harm anyone. This means telling your family and friends about your struggles. There is a great example of making amends in the Bible, with the story of David and his friend Jonathan. Jonathan's father Saul had made multiple attempts on David's life. But David had made certain promises to Jonathan, who died before those promises could be fulfilled.

David came out of the shadows of unkept promises, making amends to Jonathan's son Mephibosheth, who expected nothing from the king. Crippled and needy, Mephibosheth seemed destined to a life of misery. David stepped in and deeded to his new friend the valued property that had previously belonged to Saul. Further, he awarded him the honor of dining at the king's table.

"Making amends is a major building block to recovery."

At the heart of amends was this question: "David said, 'Is there anyone still left of the house of Saul to whom I can show kindness for Jonathan's sake?'" (2 Samuel 9:1).

It was in David's heart to make things right with those in his life. That is a major building block to recovery. That's why making amends is the ninth of the twelve steps. But not all amends are good amends. They must be heartfelt and genuine.

G.K. Chesterton said, "A stiff apology is a second insult. The injured party does not want to be compensated because he has been wronged; he wants to be healed because he has been hurt."

Today's Exercise

One of the most difficult things for a recovering addict to do is to tell his or her family and friends about the depths of the addiction. Facing those we love the most, only to tell them about a side of us that they may have never seen is both painful and therapeutic.

But from personal experience, I can assure you that when you share the news of your addiction with those closest to you, you will likely be surprised at the grace that you will receive from them. This may be the best thing that has ever happened in your relationships with those you value the most. For the first time, you will be fully known.

Telling others your story is not done for them, but for you. It's about coming out of the darkness and into the light. You are far enough into your recovery to start that process now. So make a list of family members and friends with whom you can share your story.

1. **Family members**
    a. _____
    b. _____
    c. _____
    d. _____
    e. _____

2. **Friends**
    a. _____
    b. _____
    c. _____
    d. _____
    e. _____

Day 77: Tell All

God's Word for Today

Secrecy is your addiction's best friend; confession is its worst nightmare. The brother of Jesus wrote, "Confess your sins to one another that you may be healed" (James 5:16). Confession is a building block for recovery.

Of course, we must confess our addiction and sins to God first. But in recovery, we must also admit to another human being the exact nature of our wrongs. That person may be your spouse or a trusted advisor. He or she must be someone you can trust, perhaps a fellow addict.

> *"True confession must be detailed and specific."*

In James' command we find two principles. First, our confession must be specific. Notice, James did not tell us to confess our *sin* (a general term for our fallen condition). Rather, he said to confess our sins to one another. That requires specificity. No stone is left unturned. True confession must be detailed and specific.

Second, our confession is to *people*, not God. While the importance of confession to God is undeniable (see 1 John 1:9), it cannot end there. James says that in the telling of our story we get well. It is therapeutic. It brings healing. And the more you tell your story, the quicker you will find peace and restoration.

Saint Augustine said, "The confession of evil works is the first beginning of good works." Confession to another human being is foundational for our recovery.

Today's Exercise

Research confirms that most addicts experience at least one slip or relapse after entering recovery. In a study cited by Dr. Milton Magness, it was found that only 13 percent never slip or relapse. The question for the 87 percent who do is this: Whom do I tell?

It is important in any relationship that ground rules be established from the beginning. Most spouses want to know if their husband or wife has a slip. Each person in recovery should have a battle plan in place should a slip or relapse occur. I suggest the following. Check the steps you would be willing to take in the event of a slip or relapse.

1. Tell your sponsor within 24 hours _____

2. Tell your spouse within 24 hours _____

3. Commit to at least three 12-step meetings per week for the next three months _____

4. See a therapist _____

5. Accept (in advance) any consequences set forth by your spouse _____

6. Give renewed attention to working the 12 steps _____

7. Attend a major event/conference for sex addiction _____

WEEK 12

MAINTENANCE

"My attitude is to never be satisfied. Never."
- Duke Ellington

"In flying a plane, as in other activities, it is far easier to start something than it is to finish it."
- Amelia Earhart

Day 78: Fear of Falling

God's Word for Today

I have a tremendous fear of heights. Yet, I have no problem flying on a plane. How does this make sense? A private aircraft pilot explained it to me. "What you have is not a fear of heights, but a fear of falling."

In recovery, it is good to have a fear of falling.

What I've learned from flying is that I must trust the pilot. I don't know why putting my seat tray in its upright and locked position will save me in the event of a crash, but I do it because the pilot says to. And so far, every time I put my tray table up, the plane lands safely. So there must be something to that.

"Keep doing what works, starting with meetings."

Congratulations for making it to week 12! Your goal now is to maintain what you have already found – lasting sobriety. That means you need to keep doing the things that have worked. And keep trusting the Pilot.

I have come to appreciate Matthew Perry as much for his honesty as for his acting. A recovering addict, he says, "The thing is, if I don't have sobriety, I don't have anything."

Keep doing what's working. Recovery is a journey, not a destination. I have a friend who has been sober for 25 years. His profession keeps him on the road most of the year. Though no one would know if he is working his program or not, he still attends at least one 12-step meeting every week, no matter where he is.

Jesus warned, "I am coming soon. Hold on to what you have, so that no one will take your crown" (Revelation 3:11). Keep doing what works – starting with meetings. Recovery is for life. So stay at it. And never lose your fear of falling.

Today's Exercise

Every now and then, I hear someone say something like, "I used to be an addict. But God healed me." And they drop out of recovery. While I know God can completely remove our addictive compulsions, rarely is that the case. And in each of the instances in which I have heard addicts say they were "healed," they returned to the old ways within a few weeks.

Never take your sobriety for granted. What you have spent months obtaining can be lost in five minutes. So keep doing what works – starting with attending meetings.

Below, check the things you will commit to, in order to maintain your sobriety.

1. Attend 12-step meetings _____

2. Work with my sponsor _____

3. Read recovery materials _____

4. Help others find recovery _____

5. Work the 12 steps _____

6. Connect with my Higher Power _____

7. Therapy (as needed) _____

8. Surrender to God daily _____

9. Remain desperate _____

Day 79: Gratitude

God's Word for Today

The great philosopher Willie Nelson said, "When I started counting my blessings, my whole life turned around."

I'll say something you rarely hear. Willie makes sense. The fact is, the people who have received the most blessings, who have been healed of the greatest addictions, should be the most grateful for their new lease on life.

Case in point – Mary Magdalene.

Mary was a shining example of gratitude. Once possessed by seven demons, she had been set free by Christ. And she responded with unparalleled gratitude and loyalty. When Jesus was crucified on the cross, she was there. When Jesus needed a tomb for his burial, she was there. And when he rose the third day, she was there. Mary had come to the tomb in order to offer a sacrifice of rare perfume.

> *"Happiness is not determined by how much you have, but by how much you are grateful for."*

The Bible says, "When Jesus rose early on the first day of the week, he appeared first to Mary Magdalene, out of whom he had driven seven demons" (Mark 16:9). People full of gratitude find themselves at the right place at the right time.

Zig Ziglar said, "Gratitude is the healthiest of all human emotions. The more you express gratitude for what you have, the more likely you will have even more to express gratitude for."

Happiness is not determined by how much you have, but by how much you are grateful for. And for you, that starts with recovery. Be grateful for how far you have come.

Today's Exercise

You have a lot to be thankful for. Expressing that gratitude is a key component to maintaining your sobriety. So make a list of the things you have to be grateful for, starting with your recovery. Write down some of the things you have learned and the people who have blessed you in your recovery process, including sponsors and others in your group.

1. **My blessings from recovery**
    a. _____
    b. _____
    c. _____
    d. _____
    e. _____

2. **My other blessings**
    a. _____
    b. _____
    c. _____
    d. _____
    e. _____
    f. _____
    g. _____
    h. _____
    i. _____
    j. _____

Day 80: Euphoric Recall

God's Word for Today

We are told to "take captive every thought to make it obedient to Christ" (2 Corinthians 10:5). That is the answer to today's theme: euphoric recall.

When we find solid recovery, our minds move into overdrive. One of the last waves of attack is euphoric recall, which is a flood of past images or experiences, which threaten to take over our minds – and put our sobriety at risk.

I encourage you to practice the "3-second rule." When an intrusive thought invades your mind, move on within three seconds. How? Say a prayer, read a verse, make a call.

"Lustful thoughts make collect calls. When we accept the call, it will cost us – mightily."

Let me illustrate. Back in the day, we had this thing in our house we called a "land line." It was a precursor to the modern cell phone. We called it a telephone. When someone wanted to contact us, they dialed our number, and this thing would ring. We'd pick up the receiver. And sometimes, it would be what we called a "long distance call." This one cost money. We'd hear the voice of the "operator," who would ask if we were willing to "accept" a call that was made "collect." In other words, once we knew who was trying to call us, we had about three seconds to decide whether we were willing to pay to hear what they had to say.

Lustful thoughts make collect calls. When we accept the call, it will cost us – mightily.

Aristotle said it like this: "It is the mark of an educated mind to be able to entertain a thought without accepting it."

Temptations always call collect. You will recognize the voice. And when you do, don't negotiate the price or ask what he/she wants. Just hang up – fast!

Today's Exercise

Alexandra Katehakis has offered great counsel on the subject of euphoric recall. She writes, "Addicts may engage in the euphoria that comes with recalling past sexual experiences, labeled 'euphoric recall.' They may also fantasize about some future sexual exploit. What's the outcome of these activities? The sexual experience becomes an avoidance of connection with the partner and their own feelings in the present."[15]

George Collins writes, "Euphoric recall is a function of your mind and your memory. The key is to live a more fulfilling life in the present."[16]

That is the key to defeating euphoric recall - live in the moment. Remember that you are not your mind. You are the boss. You tell your mind where to focus, not the other way around.

When sexual images threaten to become euphoric recall, determine to shift to the present. Focus on something current, such as your family, spiritual life, or plans for tomorrow.

When sexual thoughts seek to take up residency in your mind, make sure they rent and do not own. In other words, evict these thoughts before they have time to unpack their endless images into your head.

What are three things you can focus on when your mind is invaded with sexual images?

1. _____

2. _____

3. _____

---

15 Alexandra Katehakis, "Addicted to Sex: There Are No Shortcuts to Treating SA," *Psychotherapy Networker,* April, 2010, 33.
16 Collins, *Breaking the Cycle,* 40.

Day 81: Be Good to Yourself

God's Word for Today

Early in recovery, it is natural for an addict to look around the room in a 12-step meeting and conclude, "There are guys here with years of sobriety! I have so far to go!"

We need to celebrate early success in our recovery. In the Old Testament we read about the determination that led the Israelites to rebuild the Temple, their sacred place of worship. "When the builders completed the foundation of the Lord's Temple, they clashed their cymbals to praise the Lord, just as King David had prescribed" (Ezra 3:10).

"God has put before us a table at which to feast, not an altar on which to die."

Did you catch that? The builders didn't hold off on the celebration until the Temple was finished. They celebrated when the Temple was just started.

Recovery is never finished. If you wait until you have reached perfection, until you have "arrived," before you celebrate, you can leave the cymbals in the box.

The fact that you are reading this right now is something. Your 12 weeks into recovery is a big thing. In 12-step meetings, newcomers receive a 24-hour desire chip, marking their desire for one day of sobriety. Why? Because every sober day is big.

The builders of the Temple had only laid the foundation, but they paused to celebrate. By working this 12-week plan of recovery, you have laid your own foundation for a lifetime of recovery. And that is worth celebrating!

John Calvin said, "God has put before us a table at which to feast, not an altar on which to die." Go find your table today. Embrace recovery, and do something good for yourself!

Today's Exercise

Your time of recovery is worth celebrating! Just laying the foundation is a monumental achievement. Never take that for granted. It is a good idea to reward yourself for a job well done, from time to time.

Dr. Magness suggests about 120 specific hobbies you might consider, in building a healthy life and celebrating your success.[17] One of the things you can do is to schedule a monthly Recovery Day. This is a time to get away and have some fun, while focusing on recovery issues.

List some things you can do to celebrate the foundation for recovery that has already been put in place.

- _____
- _____
- _____
- _____
- _____
- _____
- _____
- _____
- _____
- _____
- _____
- _____
- _____

---

17 Magness, *Thirty Days to Hope & Freedom*, 122-123.

Day 82: Check In

God's Word for Today

Marilyn Monroe said, "I am good, but I'm no angel. I am just a small girl in a big world trying to find someone to love."

With those words, Marilyn Monroe spoke for all of us. If you struggle with compulsive behaviors, you are still a good person, locked in a struggle for sobriety and sanity. The man closest to Jesus admitted, "If we claim to be without sin, we deceive ourselves, and the truth is not in us" (1 John 1:8).

> *"If you fall short, you can find forgiveness. That's God's nature."*

You may feel awkward about bringing your recurring sins before the Lord. You may be embarrassed by the number of times you have had to deal with the same issues – issues that stubbornly refuse to go away. You may imagine that God is collecting a long list of repeated offenses to be used against you. But the truth is simple. If you recognize your mistakes and confess them to God, he will forgive you.

The goal is 100 percent sobriety – no more slips and no more relapses – ever. Never accept anything less as your goal. But if you do fall short from time to time don't kick yourself. We all continue to struggle. And God is in the business of forgiveness and restoration.

The struggle will be with you for the rest of your life – every single day. That's human nature. But if you do fall short, you can also find forgiveness. That's God's nature.

Today's Exercise

We have a second chance God. He thrives on forgiveness. But in recovery, we need to not only confess our shortcomings to him, but also those closest to us. If you are married, today's exercise is for you. Dr. Milton Magness has suggested a formula for the addict to use to stay current with his or her spouse.[18] It's called the FASTT check-in. This can be done in just a few minutes. This is an exercise that helps bring restoration and healing to the wounded spouse. Each day, you can take just a few minutes, as you check in according to the following.

F = Feelings
A = Activities in recovery
S = Sexual sobriety statement or slip report
T = Threats to sobriety
T = Tools for recovery

Magness suggests that the addict should continue this check-in practice for at least three years following his initial disclosure. It is critical that the recovering addict initiate these daily check-ins, rather than the spouse having to ask for them.

Plan the date for your first FASTT check-in.

The date of my first FASTT check-in: _____

---

18 Magness, *Stop Sex Addiction* (Las Vegas, NV: Central Recovery Press, 2013), 220.

Day 83: Sponsoring Others

God's Word for Today

We need to live lives of purpose. David said, "The Lord will vindicate me; your love, Lord, endures forever. Do not abandon the works of your hands" (Psalm 138:8).

No one lived a purposeful life better than Teddy Roosevelt. He was a cowboy, explorer, and big game hunter. He rode as a cavalry officer in the Spanish-American War. As a vice presidential candidate, he gave 673 speeches and traveled 20,000 miles. Years after his presidency, he was shot in the chest just before a scheduled speech in Milwaukee. He gave the one-hour speech anyway, then went to the hospital.

"God wants us to be difference-makers."

Asked the key to success, Roosevelt said, "Spend yourself on a worthy cause."

You can't do that if you are mired in an addiction. Make recovery your "worthy cause." Everything else can be built on that solid foundation.

Coretta Scott King said, "My story is a freedom song of struggle. It's about finding one's purpose, how to overcome fear and to stand up for causes bigger than one's self."

There you have it – from King David, President Roosevelt, and Coretta Scott King. Live life with purpose. Set your eye on the prize, then order your steps in that direction.

What is God's ultimate purpose for this life? God wants us to be difference-makers. And that fits perfectly in the process of continued recovery.

Today's Exercise

Your recovery will not be complete until you give back. You can work all the steps, enjoy successful sobriety, and check all the boxes. But the cycle is not complete until you help someone else.

You do that by becoming a sponsor. In so doing, you will find that by helping others you will help yourself. Nothing will secure your own recovery more than helping someone else to secure theirs.

Different 12-step groups maintain various standards for becoming a sponsor. Some require that every sponsor complete the 12 steps first. Others set a sobriety requirement, from one month to a full year.

You should learn the requirements of sponsorship in your group. If you are not yet sponsoring someone, ask your sponsor for guidance in this area. There are plenty of tools and resources available to help.

Because you have completed nearly three months of recovery yourself, you are learning some of the attributes God has given you that will make you an effective sponsor. List five of those attributes below.

1. _____

2. _____

3. _____

4. _____

5. _____

Day 84: Spiritual Connection

God's Word for Today

A man had a firewood factory that employed hundreds of men. He paid them well and gave them specific directions on what to do. But their work was slow and unproductive. Eventually, he had no choice. He fired the men and purchased a circular saw powered by a gas engine. In one hour, the new saw accomplished more than the men had done in a week.

The man talked to his new saw. "How can you turn out so much work? Are you sharper than the saws my men were using before?"

The saw responded, "No, I am not sharper than the other saws. The difference is the gas engine. I have a stronger power behind me. I am productive because of the power that is working through me, not because my blade is sharper."

> *"At the root of success is total surrender to God."*

The man or woman who finds successful recovery doesn't do so because he or she has a better saw. It's all about the power within. The Bible calls that power the Holy Spirit.

Jesus promised his earliest followers, "You will receive power when the Holy Spirit comes on you" (Acts 1:8).

That's the secret. It's not the sharpness of the saw, but the presence of the Spirit that counts.

That is an important lesson for men and women who have achieved a level of sobriety. It is easy to forget this is a spiritual program of recovery. At the root of success is total surrender to God. He has all the power you need. And that's good because, as with the saw, you aren't that sharp.

Today's Exercise

To maintain your sobriety, you must maintain your connection to God. That must be a daily, intentional endeavor. The basic spiritual disciplines must be a part of your daily life. Below, you will find some of the components we recommend for you to use in order to maintain your daily sobriety. Circle the ones you are either utilizing now, or are willing to utilize in the future.

1. "Recovery Minute" devotion (sign up through our ministry at TheresStillHope.org)

2. Life Recovery Bible (available from our ministry upon request)

3. 3rd Step Prayer (found in this workbook and in all 12-step literature)

4. 7th Step Prayer (found in this workbook and 12-step material)

5. Serenity Prayer (easily accessible)

6. Commitment to 24 hours of sobriety

7. Meditation

8. Journaling

FINISH STRONG

"I do the very best I know how, the very best I can, and I mean to keep on doing so until the end."
— **Abraham Lincoln**

"Don't give up at half time. Concentrate on winning the second half."
— **Paul "Bear" Bryant**

Day 85: The New You

God's Word for Today

Kierkegaard wrote, "In the understanding of the moment, never has anyone accomplished so little by the sacrifice of a consecrated life as did Jesus Christ. And yet in this same instant, eternally understood, he had accomplished all, and on that account said, 'It is finished.'"

Peter said that Jesus died to secure "the genuineness of our faith" (1 Peter 1:7).

Jesus' death was not primarily for the history books. It is more personal than that. **"Jesus paid it all."** Because Jesus died for our shortcomings, we can find victory. Freedom Is not based on what we can do, but on what he has already done.

In the nineteenth century, Elvina Hall understood this when she became the first to perform a new hymn at the Monument Street Methodist Church in Baltimore. This is the first stanza of that hymn. Perhaps you've heard of it.

> *I heard the Savior say, thy strength indeed is small.*
> *Child of weakness, watch and pray. Find in me thine all in all.*
> *Jesus paid it all, all to him I owe.*
> *Sin had left a crimson stain, he washed it white as snow.*

Two thousand years before you were born, Jesus knew you would have this disease we call sex addiction. And He knew the price of freedom would be more than you could afford. So what did he do? As the hymn says, Jesus paid it all.

Today's Exercise

Congratulations on making it to the home stretch! These final six exercises are designed to cement the recovery you have already achieved. As you read in today's devotional, Jesus paid for your recovery. But you still have work to do. You have entered into a partnership with God.

You have come a long way. For today's exercise, find a place where you can be alone. You will need two chairs. Sit in one and set the other one just in front of you. As you look at the empty chair, think about the ways you have changed since entering recovery.

The chair you start out in represents the "old you." The empty chair represents the "new you." Now, get up and go claim that chair. This is representative of the change that recovery has brought to your life. Take a minute to sit in the new chair, and pray. Thank God that even though you aren't all you're supposed to be, and though you aren't all you're going to be – you aren't what you used to be, either.

Thank God for who and what you have already become.

Day 86: 90-Day Check-Up

God's Word for Today

Is there a silver bullet to sobriety? Is there one key, one thing that will bring recovery? Is there a simple fix?

The answer is yes, but you aren't going to like what it is. It's called *discipline*.

Paul told young Timothy how to win in life. "Fight the good fight of the faith" (1 Timothy 6:12).

I've seen boxers fight and I've seen them train. The fight is determined by the training. It is the miles of roadwork and hundreds of rounds in the gym that create the successful fighter. It is what is done when no one is watching that makes the fighter great.

"Discipline is the bridge between goals and accomplishment."

In your addiction, you have found your strongest opponent. He will come at you with everything that he's got. And he keeps getting up, no matter how many times he's been down or the number of rounds you have already won. He is relentless in his attack and unyielding in his efforts. And even though you may be ahead on points, he can still take you out with a single punch in the final round.

Unless you are diligent in your preparation and disciplined in your defense. Jim Rohn was right: "Discipline is the bridge between goals and accomplishment."

If your next 90 days are to be as successful as your last 90 days, you will have to embrace the discipline that precedes each battle – discipline to go to meetings, make calls, and never give up.

Today's Exercise

In recovery, and life, we all want to finish strong. That requires maintaining the same habits that secured your sobriety in the first place. It's always helpful to do a quick check-up, to make sure your recovery is still on track. So let's go over a few of the things that got you here: going to meetings, getting a sponsor, becoming a sponsor, prayer, worship, reading recovery literature, etc.

Here's the basic truth – what it takes to achieve sobriety is the same thing it takes to *maintain* sobriety.

So let's do a 90-day check-up. Check the activities you are committed to, going forward.

- Weekly SA or SAA meeting _____

- Working with my sponsor _____

- Being or becoming a sponsor _____

- Connecting with God _____

- Making daily recovery calls _____

- Reading recovery materials _____

- Praying 3rd Step & 7th Step prayers _____

- Reaching out to newcomers in the program _____

- Other: _____

Day 87: Step 12

God's Word for Today

Saint Augustine said, "What does love look like? It has the hands to help others. It has the feet to hasten to the poor and needy. It has eyes to see misery and want. It has the ears to hear the sights and sorrows of men. That is what love looks like."

Augustine seemed to understand recovery. The best way to secure the ground you have already conquered is to help others do the same. In recovery work, that is called the 12th Step.

"Having had a spiritual awakening as the result of these steps, we tried to carry this message to sexaholics and to practice these principles in all our affairs" (Step 12).

> **"Help others achieve their dreams and you will achieve yours."**

There are many ways you can do this. The obvious answer is to become a sponsor for someone who is new to sobriety. But considering that we live in a world where sex and porn addiction are destroying millions of lives, the opportunities to make a difference are limitless.

Join a men's Bible study. It won't take long before you identify guys who struggle with this problem. Get involved in civic clubs, neighborhood groups, and hobbies. You are surrounded by those you can help. The key is to build relationships with people who don't already have it all together.

Les Brown said, "Help others achieve their dreams and you will achieve yours." This is never truer than in addiction recovery.

The writer of Hebrews nailed it: "Do not neglect to do good and to share what you have, for such sacrifices are pleasing to God" (Hebrews 13:16).

There. You have your marching orders. Now, let's get specific with today's exercise.

Today's Exercise

"Having had a spiritual awakening as a result of these steps, we tried to carry this message to sexaholics and to practice these principles in all our affairs" (Step 12).

There is a story of three men whose plane crashed in the middle of the desert. They needed water, but did not know where to find it. And they each had a gun with a single bullet. So they drew up a simple plan for survival. The men would spread out and walk in opposite directions in search of water. And the first man to discover water would fire his bullet, notifying the others where to go for the water.

Within about an hour, one of the men found water - more than he could ever drink himself. But rather than notifying the others, he set his gun down and helped himself to the water, while the others died of thirst.

That is an illustration of the sex addict who finds recovery, but does not share his success with others in need.

You are better than that. What you have found, you must share. You have had a spiritual awakening as a result of these steps, so now it is time for you to carry this message to sexaholics and to practice these principles in all your affairs.

There are many ways to practice the 12th Step. Identify one, and write it down here:

_____
_____
_____
_____

Day 88: Living Amends

God's Word for Today

Dr. George Simon is a leading expert on manipulators and the author of *In Sheep's Clothing*. He cites four marks of true change: acknowledgment of a wrong, the willingness to confess it, the willingness to abandon it, and the willingness to make restitution.

Did you catch that last one – restitution?

When Zacchaeus – who made government tax fraud a sport – came to faith in Christ, it changed everything. Zacchaeus quickly raced through the first three steps. He acknowledged that he had been robbing people of their taxes. He confessed it openly. And he committed to never doing it again. But then came the difference-maker.

"We know we have become sober because we have quit acting out. And we know we are in recovery because we make restitution."

"Zacchaeus stood up and said to the Lord, 'Look, Lord! Here and now I give half of my possessions to the poor, and if I have cheated anybody out of anything, I will pay back four times the amount'" (Luke 19:8).

We know we have become sober because we have quit acting out. And we know we are in recovery because we make restitution. It's called *making amends*. It's the 9th step in 12-Step work. But it doesn't have to wait. Like Zacchaeus, you can start right away.

There are likely people or institutions you have harmed, but to go to them directly would cause more harm than good. The answer is not to do nothing, but to make what we call indirect or living amends.

Today's Exercise

There are three kinds of amends: direct, indirect, and living. Direct amends are made directly to the person harmed. We try to do that in person, if possible.

But sometimes, making such amends is either impossible or unwise. In such cases, we can make indirect amends. For example, if you spent time viewing porn on work hours, you can put in free overtime. If you have harmed a person you should not approach, you might give to their favorite charity.

Living amends are available to all of us. By living a life of purity – and helping others find recovery as well – you make living amends. This should be a lifelong endeavor.

Below, make a list of five people or institutions to whom you can make indirect or living amends. And write one way you can do this.

- Person or institution: _____
  How to make amends: _____
  _____

- Person or institution: _____
  How to make amends: _____
  _____

- Person or institution: _____
  How to make amends: _____
  _____

- Person or institution: _____
  How to make amends: _____
  _____

- Person or institution: _____
  How to make amends: _____
  _____

Day 89: Stay at It!

God's Word for Today

Martin Lloyd Jones said, "There is nothing which so certifies the genuineness of a man's faith as his patient endurance, his keeping on steadily in spite of everything."

We all want to experience recovery as quickly as possible. It's hard to be patient. But we didn't get into our mess overnight. And it takes time to get out of the ditch. The first 90 days of recovery are the hardest. But you have only just begun.

The key to tomorrow's sobriety is today's work. So keep doing the things that you know work.

Attend meetings, call others in the program, read recovery materials. If you continue to do these things, great blessings will come to you and those around you.

> *"The key to tomorrow's sobriety is today's work."*

You are probably familiar with a man named Job. In the Old Testament book that bears his name, we read how he lost everything. But most of us forget to read the rest of the story.

In the final chapter, we read, "The Lord blessed the latter part of Job's life more than the former part. He had 14,000 sheep, 6,000 camels, 1,000 yoke of oxen, and 1,000 donkeys" (Job 42:12).

Did you catch that? "The Lord blessed the latter part of Job's life more than the former part."

Dale Carnegie observed, "Most of the important things in the world have been accomplished by people who have kept on trying when there seemed to be no hope at all."

Elton Trueblood said, "Our life is a gift from God. What we do with that life is our gift to God." By giving the rest of your life to God, you can claim this promise: the best is yet to come.

Today's Exercise

Like Job, your ending can be better than your start. God is not finished with you yet. And there is one truth I have come to embrace in recovery above all else: *What God allows, God redeems.*

God could have protected you from your addiction. He could have miraculously taken away your compulsions. But God has allowed you to walk this journey for two reasons: to learn to trust in him and so that you can help others.

Five years before Job received the great blessings of God, he likely had no idea what was coming his way. The same may be true for you. There are some blessings you cannot predict. But while you can't predict what will happen *to* you, you do have a voice in what happens *in* you.

This will be a fun exercise. Think ahead five years. As you work your recovery plan, what might your life look like in five years? List five things below. They may be your goals for recovery, restored relationships, or anything else that you can only attain through healthy recovery.

1. _____

2. _____

3. _____

4. _____

5. _____

Day 90: You Win!

God's Word for Today

The Battle of Waterloo was fought on June 18, 1815, near the city of Waterloo in present day Belgium. All of England knew that the Duke of Wellington was leading the British forces against the French Emperor, Napoleon Bonaparte, in this epic battle. A ship signaled news of the outcome of the battle to a man on top of Winchester Cathedral. The message consisted of three words: "Wellington defeated Napoleon."

But the fog rolled in before the man at the Cathedral saw the third word. Therefore, the message that went out across England was, "Wellington defeated." The British thought they had lost the decisive battle, which they had actually won.

> **"We don't live for victory; we live from victory."**

Sometimes, we get mixed messages. In your 90 days of recovery, there have probably been many times when you felt defeated. When the temptations hit hardest, when fantasy attacks, and when you feel especially weak, remember that this battle is not your own. Our Higher Power has already defeated the enemy. We don't live *for* victory; we live *from* victory.

Sun Tzu had it right: "The supreme art of war is to subdue the enemy without fighting."

Your job today is to surrender. Tomorrow, do it again. Then, embrace this passage of Scripture. "Give glory to him who is able to keep you from falling" (Jude 24).

Congratulations on making it through 90 days. Remember, recovery is not about perfection, but progress. And you have made great progress. But the journey has just begun . . .

Today's Exercise

It's time for a Recovery Day! This is a day set apart to celebrate your progress in recovery, and to refocus on the things that need fresh attention. Set aside a day within the next week or so to get away, read recovery materials, pray, attend a meeting, journal, and recommit yourself to the things that fuel your recovery the most.

Again, congratulations! Now, let's plan your special day.

Recovery Day date: _____

Rewarding activities for the day:
- a. _____
- b. _____
- c. _____

Recovery activities I will focus on for the future:
- a. _____
- b. _____
- c. _____
- d. _____
- e. _____

ADDITIONAL RESOURCES

Twelve-Step Programs for Sex Addiction

    Sexaholics Anonymous (www.sa.org)
    Sex Addicts Anonymous (www.sexaa.org)
    Sex and Love Addicts Anonymous (www.slaafws.org)
    Sexual Recovery Anonymous (www.sexualrecovery.org)
    Castimonia (www.castimonia.org)

Twelve-Step Programs for Spouses of Sex Addicts

    S-ANON (www.sanon.org)
    Co-Dependents of Sex Addicts (www.cosa.recovery.org)

Intensive Outpatient Sex Addiction Services

    Hope Quest (www.hopequest.org)
    Hope & Freedom Counseling Services (www.hopeandfreedom.com)
    Sexual Recovery Institute (www.sexualrecovery.com)

Christ-Centered Workshops

    Bethesda (www.bethesdaworkshops.org)
    Faithful & True (www.faithfulandtrue.com)
    Be Broken Ministries (www2.bebroken.com)

SUGGESTED READINGS

Alcoholics Anonymous, Fourth Edition. (2002). New York, NY: Alcoholics Anonymous Word Services, Inc.

Arterburn, S., & Stoeker, F. (2002). *Every Man's Battle*. Colorado Springs, CO: WaterBrook Press.

Carnes, P. (2001). *Out of the Shadows*: Starting sexual and relationship recovery. Carefree, AZ: Gentle Path Press.

Carnes, P. (2009), *Recovery Zone*. Carefree, AZ: Gentle Path Press.

Carnes, P. (2015). *Facing the Shadows* (3rd ed.). Center City, NV: Hazelden.

Chester, T. (2010). *Closing the Window: Steps to Living Porn-Free*. Westmont, IL: Intervarsity Press.

Clinton, T., & Laaser, M. (2010). *Sexuality & Relationship Counseling*. Ada, MI: Baker Books.

Clinton, T., & Laaser. M. (2015). *The Fight of Your Life: Manning up to the Challenge of Sexual Integrity*. Shippensberg, PA: Destiny Image Publishers.

Collins, G. (2010). *Breaking the Cycle*. Oakland, CA: New Harbinger Publications, Inc.

Dobberfuhl, D. (2011). *Overcoming Addiction*. Brigham City, UT: Walnut Springs Press.

Dougherty, J. (2018). *Grace-Based Recovery*. Greensboro, NC: New Growth Press.

Laaser, M. (2004). *Healing the Wounds of Sexual Addiction*. Grand Rapids, MI: Zondervan.

Magness, M. (2011). *Thirty Days to Hope & Freedom*. Las Vegas, NV: Central Recovery Press.

Magness, M. (2012). *I can stop: The 30-Day Solution to Sex Addiction*. DVD Series. H&F Media.

Magness, M. (2013). *Stop Sex Addiction*. Las Vegas, NV: Central Recovery Press.

Magness, M., & Means, M. (2017). *Real Hope, True Freedom*. Las Vegas, NV: Central Recovery Press.

Schneider, J., & Corley, D. (2012). *Disclosing Secrets: A Sex Addict's Guide for When, To Whom, And How Much to Reveal*. Seattle, WA: CreateSpace Independent Publishing.

Sexaholics Anonymous. (2008). Nashville, TN: Author.

Sex Addicts Anonymous, Second Edition. (2008). Houston, TX: Author.

Weiss, D. (2015). *101 Freedom Exercises*. Colorado Springs, CO: Heart2Heart.

ABOUT THE AUTHOR

Mark and Beth Denison are the founders and directors of There's Still Hope, a Christ-centered sex addiction recovery ministry. With a comprehensive focus on addicts, spouses, and pastors, TSH provides multi-faceted resources: personal coaching, group work, speaking in churches and schools, daily online devotions, and printed materials.

For 30 years, Mark served as a senior pastor to three different churches in his home state of Texas. He also served three terms as Board Chair at his alma mater, Houston Baptist University, and as a chaplain to the Houston Rockets for five seasons. He has earned four degrees, including a doctorate (Southwestern Baptist Theological Seminary) and two master's degrees, the last of which is in addiction recovery (Liberty University). Mark is an active member of the American Association of Christian Counselors.

Mark and Beth are proud parents of one son, who is also involved in ministry. They live in Bradenton, Florida, where they enjoy the Florida beaches and serve faithfully in their local church.

Mark has authored three other books: *The Daily Walk, Porn in the Pew*, and *365 Days to Sexual Integrity*.

www.ingramcontent.com/pod-product-compliance
Lightning Source LLC
Chambersburg PA
CBHW062206080426
42734CB00010B/1811